Man and Mahatma

Man and Mahatma

J. M. Mehta

PUSTAK MAHAL®

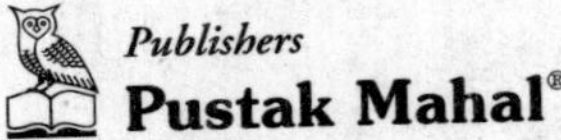

Publishers
Pustak Mahal®

Administrative office and sale centre

J-3/16 , Daryaganj, New Delhi-110002
☎ 23276539, 23272783, 23272784 • *Fax:* 011-23260518
E-mail: info@pustakmahal.com • *Website:* www.pustakmahal.com

Branches
Bengaluru: ☎ 080-22234025 • *Telefax:* 080-22240209
E-mail: pustak@airtelmail.in • pustak@sancharnet.in
Mumbai: ☎ 022-22010941, 022-22053387
E-mail: rapidex@bom5.vsnl.net.in
Patna: ☎ 0612-3294193 • *Telefax:* 0612-2302719
E-mail: rapidexptn@rediffmail.com

ISBN 978-81-223-1414-4

Edition: 2013

Printed at : Param Offsetters, Okhla, Delhi

Preface

It may sound ironical that the man on whom we bestowed the grand title of the "FATHER OF THE NATION" and who made the greatest contribution in India's struggle for freedom, seems to have been almost forgotten by most us, especially by the politicians of our country. It may perhaps be surprising to know if the majority of our common folk, in particular, those who belong to the younger generation may wonder, WHO IS GANDHI?

Inspite of what has been said above, Gandhi Ji had a ray of revival, most astonishingly through bollywood and by some faint coverage in the media. The popularity of the blockbuster hit film LAGE RAHO MUNNABHAI produced some curiosity in the young minds to know more about Gandhi Ji. The film made some solid contribution in revitalizing the interest in GANDHIGIRI and Gandhi Ji. It is interesting to note that Gandhi's progeny who had mostly stayed out of active politics, plunged into publication of book on him. Two books written by his descendants were published during 2007. A large number of biographies and some other books on Gandhi Ji are also available in the market. But, most of these are either bulky or quite costly and hence, within the reach of only few.

Different writers have viewed Gandhi Ji from different perspectives. Some found in him a deeply religions person and called him a SAINT. Some thought he was a shrewd social and political strategist, while some felt he was a remarkable leader of the country.

Roman Rolland, the French Nobel laureate, portrayed him as a saint who had all the Christian virtues and casually mentioned Gandhi Ji as a 'LIVING CHRIST'.

Rabindranath Tagore, the Indian Nobel laureate, once said that Gandhi Ji was prodigiously interesting for an artist to study, extremely complex, a mixture of grandeur and pettiness, and a lofty political personality as well.

Winston Churchill, simply called him a Naked Fakir. Several other opinion might have been expressed about him; but to the taming millions of India, he was an enduring, loving, caring and sharing BAPU, to gain whose blessing and darshan they flocked in large numbers. All consider Gandhi Ji as the greatest man of the 21st century. He rose from the mundane to the superhuman level by virtue of his innate qualities, original thoughts, purity of mind and sublime actions and achieved the highest greatness of a Mahatma (which means a great soul) from an ordinary beginning.

My interest grew in Gandhi Ji when I started reading his autobiography *'My Experiments with Truth'*. Thereafter, I have studied lot of literature on him and consequently have accumulated considerable thoughts and informations relating to his life and personality. As a result of this interest and my insatiable quest, I have found it fit and desirable to write a small book which throws sufficient light on the man who had an ordinary start but gradually rose to become Mahatma.

In this small book, I have made sincere attempts to bring the great man and his thoughts within an easy reach of the common educated people. I am confident that the general reader will derive great benefit and inspiration from the incidents and thoughts of Gandhi Ji as depicted in this book. I also wish to add that this book is not intended to offer another biography or any detailed exposition of his political cause to the readers. As a matter of fact, the narration of most of his political life and activities in India has been left out intentionally. The emphasis, as the title of the book shows, is on the glimpses of the Man and the Mahatma.

J.M.MEHTA

J-186-SAKET

NEW DELHI-110017.

Contents

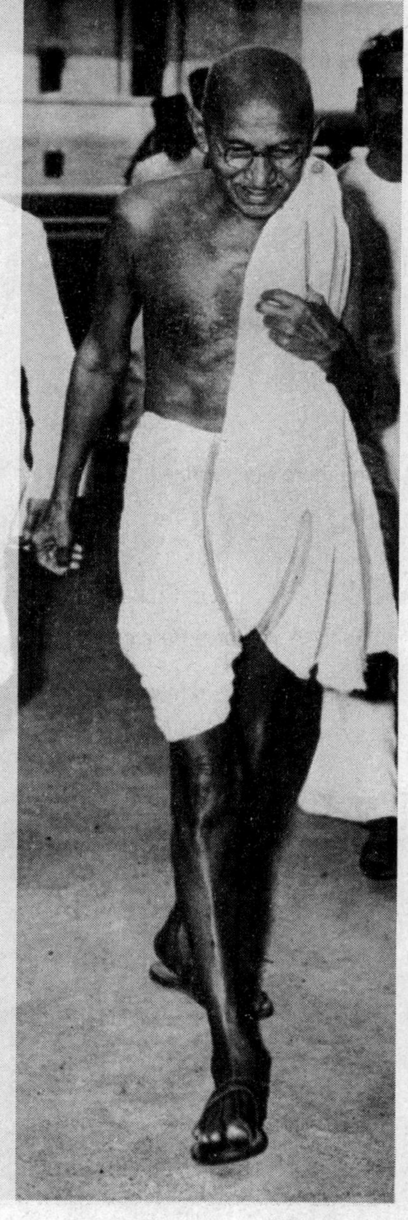

Part-III

Part-IV

Part-V

Part-VI

India of Gandhi's Dreams

I shall strive from a constitution which will release India from all thralldom and patronage, and give her, if need be, the right to sin. I shall work for an India in which the poorest shall feel that it is their country, in whose making they have an effective voice, an India in which there shall be no high class and low class of people; an India in which all communities shall live in perfect harmony. There can be no room in such an India for the curse of untouchability, or the curse of intoxicating drinks and drugs. Women will enjoy the same rights as men. We shall be at peace with the rest of the world. This is the India of my dreams.

– Mohandas Karamchand Gandhi

G.K. Gokhale on Gandhi Ji

"Gentlemen, it is one of the privileges of my life that I know Mr. Gandhi intimately and I can tell you that a purer, a nobler, a braver and a more exalted spirit has never moved on the earth."

Mr. Gokhale, the great Indian leader of his time, spoke this at the Lohore session of Indian National Congress in 1909.

Einstein on Gandhi Ji

"Generations to come will scarce believe that such a one as this ever in flesh and blood walked upon this earth."

"I believe that Gandhi's view were the most enlightened of all the political men of our time. We should strive to do things in his spirit: not to use violence for fighting for our cause, but by non-participation in anything you believe is evil."

Part - 1

- Early Life
- Stay in England and Return to India
- Gandhi in South Africa
- Experiences in South Africa
- Turning Point in the Life of Gandhi
- Some Powerful Influences on Gandhi

Early Life

Gandhi whose full name is Mohandas Karamchand Gandhi, was born on October 2, 1869 at Porbandar, a small town in Kathiawar (Gujarat), situated on the Western coast of India. His family belonged to the Bania caste, seems to have been originally grocers. The family rose in status when Gandhi's grand father, Uttamchand Gandhi and became the Dewan (Prime Minister) of Porbandar. He was a strict man of strict principles.

Gandhi's father Karamchand Gandhi, who was the fifth son of Uttamchand, also became the Dewan of Porbandar. He was truthful, brave, generous but short tempered. To a certain extent, he might have been given to carnal pleasures as he married four times, having lost his wife each time by death.

But he was able, incorruptible and earned a name for strict impartiality in his family as well as outside. Being a religious person, he was a regular visitor to temples. He used to read religious books, the Gita being his most favourite. Gandhi was the youngest son from his last wife, Putlibai Gandhi, who was deeply religious, gentle and devout, strict in her observance of rituals of fast and prayer. She would not take her meals without saying daily prayers and would also take hard vows and keep them without fail. She left a deep impression on the mind of Gandhi who had great respect for her.

In his own words 'the outstanding impression my mother has left on my memory is that of saintliness.' She was a lady of great common sense and was well informed about able matters of state.

Gandhi's father, though well placed, never had any ambition of accumulating wealth and left very small property to the family. He did not have much education but had rich experience of practical affairs that helped him in the solution of most intricate problems in managing hundreds of men.

Gandhi was born to such parents. Being the youngest child in the family, he was the most lovable of the family. His mother and elder sister took good care of him. The family affectionately called him 'MONIYA'. A nurse was also engaged for him and he had great attachment for her. But her mother for whom he had great reverence, gave him the warmest affection. The love and care which Gandhi received during his early age, became a part of his mental make-up during later life.

Gandhi spent his childhood in Porbander. As a child, he was sweet tempered, but timid and afraid of ghosts. He was shy and avoided social circle. His books were his main companions though he did not show great aptitude for studies. In his own words 'his intellect must have been sluggish and memory raw'. It was with many difficulties that he got through the multiplication tables. He ran back home as soon as the school was over as he was afraid lest others should make fun of him.

He attended a primary and then a high school in Rajkot, where the family moved from Porbander when his father became a member of the Rajasthan court. Earlier, he had attended an elementary school in Porbander.

As a student he was mediocre, shy of company and lacked any interest for games because of his poor physique. But, he loved to walk in the morning and this habit he followed throughout his life. Gandhi himself, did not have any high regard of his ability in studies and used to feel surprised whenever he won any prize or even scholarship.

Although he was not very fond of studies, he jealously guarded his character. Any rebuke was unbearable to him. Once when

A young Gandhi ji

he received corporal punishment, he wept piteously not because it hurt him physically, but because he felt ashamed of the fact that he was considered fit for punishment!

Ghandhi remained at school up to his sixteenth year where all sorts of subjects were taught except religion. But he kept on picking up values from his home and environment. He inherited purity from his mother. The conviction of truth and morality took deep roots in him.

During his early childhood, he does not remember to have told a lie, neither to his teachers nor his school mates. When he saw a performance of the play of HARISH GHANDRA, by a travelling dramatic company, he was greatly impressed by it. Truth became the sole objective of his life and it grew in magnitude every day. He also happened to read a book *'Shravana Pitribhakti'* which was purchased by his father. This was a play about Shravana devotion to his parents. Gandhi read this book with infuse interest and was very much influenced by its contents.

At the age of thirteen, while still studying in school, Gandhi was married to Kasturba. He, later in life, pitied himself for having been married at such an early age. His marriage at that age did not mean anything more than good clothes to wear, and a strange girl to play with. The newly weds behaved like 'married children' in a play. On the first night of their wedding, the two innocent children, who knew nothing about sex were put together into the pool of married life! Both were very shy and too nervous to face each other. They were coached by relatives but the coaching did not carry them far. The carnal desire came much later.

Gandhi and his wife kasturba, who was daughter of a Porbander merchant, were around the same age. After a period of initial shyness and nervousness, they gradually began to know each other and talk freely together.

At the time of his marriage Gandhi had read a few pamphlets in which conjugal love thrift, child marriages and other such topics were discussed. He learnt a few things from these readings. Lifelong faithfulness to the wife inculcated in these pamphlets remained ingrained in his heart, as the duty of the husband. He, therefore, soon assumed the authority of a husband. He said to himself, "If i should be pledged to the faithful to my wife, she should also be pledged to be faithful to me." This thought made him a jealous husband and sowed the seeds of bitterness between him and his wife.

Gandhi did not like kasturba to go out without his permission, but as she was of an independent nature, she would do so, whenever she liked and this would upset him. Consequently, sometimes they would not speak to each other for days. Despite all these small bickelings, Gandhi was passionately fond of his wife and even at school, he would think of her. At night, he would keep her awake late with his idle gossips. Late in life, he regarded his premature sensual behaviour with shame and regret.

In school, Gandhi did not take part in any exercise or sports, before these were made compulsory. One main reason for this dislike was his keen desire to serve as a nurse to his ailing father. He also lost one year because of his marriage. Studies became more difficult for him, as English became the medium of instruction in most subjects, from the fourth standard. He also found Geometry difficult as it was a new subject and the medium was English. However, later as his interest grew in this subject, he found it easy. Sanskrit proved a hard task, as there was a lot to be memorized in it. Gandhi also suffered from another deficiency which was bad handwriting. Somehow, he got the notion that good handwriting was not a necessary part of education. But, later he realized that good handwriting was a necessary part of education and he also tried to improve but it was too late then.

At the high school, Gandhi came under the influence of a Muslim boy. Sheikh Mehtab, who was a few years senior, tall, well built and a good athlete. Gandhi regarded him as a faithful friend and tried to emulate him and started eating meat under his influence. This boy could run long distances and was adept in high and long jumping. He was physically much stronger, hardier and daring and his exploits cast a spell over Gandhi. His example created a strong desire in Gandhi to be like him.

Gandhi was physically weak and was also haunted by the fear of thieves, ghosts and serpents. His friend knew all these weaknesses and therefore goaded Gandhi to meat eating to gain strength and courage. His arguments spread over a long period impressed Gandhi which took him to meat eating in secret in the company of his friend. Gandhi's parents were staunch Vaishnavas, who won't touch meat.

Initially, Gandhi found goat's meat as tough as leather and simply could not eat it. He was sick and had to leave off eating, and had a very bad night afterwards. In sleep, he would dream as if a live goat was bleeding inside him and he would jump up full of guilt and remorse. But then he would remind himself that meat eating was necessary to become strong. Meanwhile, his friend would cook various delicious dishes with meat and Gandhi started relishing meat dishes. This went on for about an year but not more than half a dozen meat-feasts were enjoyed due to financial difficulty.

Whenever Gandhi had these meat-feasts outside, he wond'nt have dinner at home. His mother would naturally enquire about the reason for not taking food and Gandhi would devise some excuses like, 'I have no appetite or there is something wrong with my digestion'. This was, perhaps, the only time when he lied to his mother. While Gandhi indulged in these secret meat-feasts, he was pricked by a sense of guilt as his family was strict vegetarian. He therefore, decided to stop eating meat and frankly conveyed his decision to his friend.

The same friend, once led Gandhi to a brothel but overpowered by a strong feeling of guilt, he could not do what he was expected to do. Having lost her patience, the woman showed him the door and insulted him. Gandhi was, thus, saved from the sinful act, by sheer grace of God. Earlier, Gandhi had also picked up the bad habit of smoking. However, all such bad influences were abandoned due to prick of conscience and due to good fortune of Gandhi. Gandhi also became fond of smoking in the company of a relative. They both imagined some pleasure in emitting clouds of smoke from the mouth. He also wanted to copy the smoking habit of his uncle.

As they had no money to buy cigarettes, they started smoking stumps of cigarettes thrown by the uncle. Then they started stealing coins from the servants' pocket money to buy cigarettes. As this did not satisfy them, they decided to commit suicide in sheer disgust, but their courage failed them. Sometime later, Gandhi stole a piece of gold from his brother's amulet. But his conscience again pricked him and he resolved never to steal again and also decided to confess his fault to his father. Since he could not do so due to lack of courage and fear, so he wrote out the confession and handed it to his father. In that he confessed his guilt, asked for adequate punishment and also sought his forgiveness. He also pledged never to steal in future. His hand was trembling as he handed over his confession to his father who was ailing and confined to bed then, he sat opposite to him.

His father read the confession and tears rolled down his cheeks. His father closed his eyes and tore up the note while Gandhi cried sensing the agony of his father. In his father's sublime act of silent forgiveness, Gandhi learnt an object lesson in Ahimsa. Instead of being angry, he found his father wonderfully peaceful. Gandhi's clean confession and firm pledge made his father to love his son more.

Gandhi was still in school, when his father was bed-ridden, suffering from fistula. His mother, he himself and an old servant were his attendants. Gandhi performed the duties of a nurse. Every night he massaged his legs and went to sleep only when asked by his father or after he had fallen asleep. He served his father with great love and in the spirit of real service and duty. However, while he was engaged in the willing act of service to his father his mind always wandered around the bed room were his wife slept. Gandhi could not restrain himself and he was glad to be relieved of his duty and went straight to his wife.

The condition of Gandhi's ailing father grew worse day by day. One dreadful night when Gandhi was serving his father, his uncle offered to relieve him and he went straight to the bed room. He woke her up but after five or six minutes, there was a knock at the door. His father expired while Gandhi was in bed with his wife. Gandhi felt deeply ashamed and miserable, as he could not be with his father in his last moments. This was the shame due to his carnal desire even at the critical hour when his father was dying. Gandhi could never forget or efface this stigma.

After passing matriculation examination in 1887, Gandhi joined a college at Bhavnagar. He could not pursue his studies there as he could not follow and take interest in progression's lectures. So, at the end of the first term, he returned back home. An old family friend and adviser suggested him that he should be sent to England for higher studies to become a barrister. Gandhi liked this idea and obtained his mother's permission after taking a vow of avoiding wine, woman and meat in England. The finance to go to England was arranged with the left of his brother. But his caste people were greatly agitated over his going abroad, as none from the caste had gone to England till then and Gandhi's visit to abroad was unacceptable to them. However, Gandhi resolved to go abroad against their wishes. He was, therefore, declared outcaste. But this did not deter Gandhi from going to England.

Stay in England and Return to India

At the age of eighteen, Gandhi went to England where he found everything strange, the people, the ford, their ways, the etiquette etc. In view of his vegetarian vow, eating food, which he found tasteless, was a problem. He would travel ten or twelve miles each day to eat in a cheap restaurant.

One day, he found a vegetarian restaurant and ate to his fill. There he found books in support of vegetarianism after reading which he became a vegetarian by his own choice. Vegetarianism at that time was a new cult in England. He joined a Vegetarian Society in England and became a member of its Executive Committee. There he came in contact with the pillars of vegetarianism and started his own experiments in dietetics. He stopped taking sweets and condiments which he had brought from India. As a result of his experiments, he learnt that the real seat of taste was not the tongue but the mind. There experiments were conducted from the point of view of hygiene and economy. Full of zeal for vegetarianism, he started a vegetarian hub in the locality where he lived and worked for the spread of his mission with the help of local supporters.

Although Gandhi was elected to the Executive Committee of the Vegetarian Society and also regularly attended its meetings, yet he could not express his thoughts and always felt tongue-tied. He could not muster courage to speak, due to his shyness which was retained throughout his stay in England. Even his last effort to make a public speech in England, which was on the virge of his departure for home, was not successful and he made himself ridiculous. However, except being an object of public laughter, his shyness in speaking had been his disadvantage. Instead, his hesitancy in speech tought him the economy of words. Experience also tought him that silence was part of the spiritual discipline of a votary of truth.

It was in England that Gandhi became acquainted with various streams of religious thought. Here he met theosophists and in their company, read Sir Edwin Arnold's translation of the Gita. *'The Song Celestial'* left a deep impression on his mind. He regarded it as the book par excellence for the knowledge of truth. He also red *'The light of Asia'* written by Edwin Arnold.

There he also met Madame Blavatsky and Mrs. Besant. He also read farmer's book *'Key to Theosophy'* which inspired him to read books on Hinduism. He also came across some good Christians and became acquainted with some portions of the Bible. He was much impressed by the '*Sermon on the Mount*'. After reading these book, he tried to unify their teachings and concluded that renunciation was the highest form of religion.

It was in England, that he read Carlyle's *'Heroes and Hero-worship'* and Mrs. Besant's book *'How I became a Theosophist'*. He also read a book on Asterisms but had no effect on him. As a result of his readings, Gandhi got some acquaintance of religions of the world, but it was not enough and he discovered that religious knowledge was never futile, as distinguished from experience. He did not then know the essence of religion or of God. He understood that it was God who saved him on different occasions of his trial. He also realized the value of worship and pray. For him, worship was not mere eloquence or lip-homage. It springs from the heart and prayer needs no speech. He had no doubt that prayer is an unfailing means of cleansing the heart if it is combined with the utmost humility.

In 1890, from England, Gandhi went to see Paris. There he saw the great exhibition, the Eiffel Tower and the ancient churches. He saw Paris, mostly on foot with the help of a guide map and managed everything very economically. He found the grandeur and peacefulness of ancient churches unforgettable. He admired the wonderful church of Notre Dame with its beautiful sculpture and elaborate decoration but did not find any art in Eiffel Tower. He considered it as the toy of the exhibition and a novelty of unique discussion.

Gandhi had gone to England to become a barrister. He found the curriculum of study easy. It took him about nine months of hard labour to go through the common law of England. He passed his examination and was called to the bar on the June 10, 1891. He enrolled himself in the high court on the June 11 and sailed for India, the next day.

On return to India, Gandhi found it difficult to practice law. He had read the law but did not know how to apply it professionally. While he studied law in England, practically he knew nothing about the Indian law. As such he found himself quite helpless and was ever doubtful about earning a living by the legal profession. Meanwhile, Gandhi's mother had died while he was still in England but the sad news was not conveyed to him. He learnt about it on return to Bombay and the news was a severe shock to him. Here, he met Raichandbhai who was a man of great character and learning and Gandhi was very much impressed by him. He found refuge in him, in his moments of spiritual crisis.

Gandhi's brother who had great desire for wealth, name and fame, had built high hopes on him. He had expected Gandhi to have roaring practice which did not happen. As he hardly had the legal knowledge of a qualified Vakil, it was not found advisable to practice in Rajkot. On the advice of some friends, he started his legal practice in Bombay

Mahatma Gandhi with his elder brother

but could not succeed. It was impossible for him, without income, to get along in Bombay for more than four or five months. This is how he found the barrister's profession a bad job, on his return to India. Even his first attempt to conduct a case in the court failed and he was disappointed.

He, therefore, decided not to take up any more cases, until he found it fit to conduct them. Since, he was good at English and also loved to teach this language, he thought of taking up a teacher's job, so that he could have some income. He applied for a teacher's job, as he came across an advertisement for an English teacher, in the newspaper. But he could not get the job, as he was not a graduate.

As there was no other source of income in Bombay, Gandhi decided to settle in Rajkot, where his brother was a party leader and he could give him some work of drafting applications. Thus, after a stay of six month's in Bombay, Gandhi returned to Rajkot and was able to earn a modest income by drafting petitions and preparing briefs for other lawyers. He returned from England with high hopes, but found the practice of law in India, a frustrating experience. He was, thus, greatly dejected and did not know what to do.

In the meantime, he received an offer of work in South Africa, from a firm in Porbandar, who had a big case pending in a court there. The case had been going on for a long time. Gandhi gladly accepted the offer which was a God sent for him. He did not go there as a barrister but as an employee of the firm to advise and help them in the firm's correspondence and other connected matters. He sailed for Durban in April 1893, leaving behind his wife and two children.

Since, his return from England, he and his wife had not lived longer together. He, therefore, feel the pain of parting with his wife. But the attraction of job in South Africa made the separation bearable. As he left Rajkot for Bombay for his voyage overseas, he consoled his wife by saying that they would meet again in a year. Gandhi arrived in Durban towards the end of May, 1893.

In this chapter, we have briefly provided information about Gandhi's early life, parentage, education in India and England, besides some experiences of his professional career in India, before he left for South Africa for the first time in 1893. He was then around twenty-four years of age, was married, had become a barrister and had two children.

At that time, there was hardly any inkling that this man, who was then just struggling to earn his livelihood, would one day scale greater heights to become the 'FATHER OF THE NATION' and rise to the exceptional glory of becoming a Mahatma (Great Soul) from a humble level.

In the next chapter, we shall briefly describe his life and experiences in South Africa. The experiences and incidents encountered there formed an influential part of the process which ultimately led to making him a Mahatma.

Gandhi in South Africa

When Gandhi reached Durban, the port of Natal in South Africa, he was received by his host, Abdulla Sheth. As the ship arrived at the port, he watched the people and observed that Indians were not held with much respect there. The foreign white settlers there who knew Abdulla, behaved towards him in a manner that reflected of snobbishness which stung Gandhi, although, Abdullah was used to it. Gandhi wore a frock coat and a turban and his dress marked him out from other Indian. People saw him with some curiosity.

A few days after his arrival in Durban, Gandhi was escorted to see the Durban court. There he was introduced to several people and was seated next to the firm's attorney. The magistrate looked at Gandhi and kept staring at him and finally asked him to remove the turban. This was perhaps in keeping with the practice that the British people would take off their hats while entering the court. But it was a different case with the turban which was worn constantly while at work or outside. Gandhi refused to remove turban and left the court.

In a few days, Gandhi noticed that Indians there were divided into different groups. One was that of Muslim merchants, the other of Hindus and yet another of Paris origin. The largest group comprised of Tamil, Telugu and North Indian indentured and freed labourers. The indentured labourers were those who went there on five years contract. The Indians were generally called as 'Coolies'.

Gandhi wrote to the press, about the incident of turban in the Durban court and defended his right of wearing a turban. This matter was much discussed in local papers and Gandhi got an unexpected advertisement in South Africa, within a few days of his arrival there. Some described him as an 'unwelcome visitor' while others supported him. However, his turban stayed with him.

A few days later, Gandhi had to go to Pretoria, as required by the firm. A first class seat was booked for him in a train. The train reached Maritzburg at night. A passenger came and he became disturbed to see Gandhi, a coloured man, in the first class compartment. He immediately went out and brought two officials. One of them asked Gandhi to go to the van compartment. Gandhi refused saying that he had a first class ticket. The official replied 'that makes no difference! You must leave and go to the van compartment'. Gandhi said 'At Durban, I was allowed to travel in this compartment. I, therefore, insist on travelling in it.'

The official insisted 'No, you won't! You must leave or I will call a police constable to push you out!' Gandhi refused to get out of his own accord. Then a constable was called who took Gandhi by loud and pushed him out of the compartment with his baggage.

Gandhi did not go to the van compartment and the train steamed away. He spent the night at Martizburg station. He took the next available train to Pretoria. En route he had to travel by a stage-coach and then again by train to reach Pretoria. During the journey, he had to encounter more hardships due to racial discrimination. He learnt from the stories narrated by other Indian merchants that what happened with him was nothing unusual and such hardships suffered by them were only a symptom of the deep disease of colour prejudice.

The First Public Speech

After reaching Pretoria, Gandhi called a meeting of Indians there, in order to acquaint them with the hardships and adverse circumstances in that region. It was the first public speech of his life. In his speech, he exhorted them to obscene truthfulness in business. He strongly contested the prevailing view among the business community that truth was not practicable in business. He also stressed the point that their responsibility to be truthful was all the more greater in a foreign country, as their conduct would be gauged as the measure of that of the millions of their fellow beings.

He also drew their attention towards their insanitary habits, as compared with those of Englishmen living around them. He also laid stress on ignoring all communal distinctions, such as Hindus, Muslims, Parisians etc. In conclusion, he suggested the formation of an association to project the hardships faced by Indian settlers to the local authorities. In this regard, he offered his help and service as much as possible. Later, such meetings was held regularly and there was free exchange of ideas. As a result of their meeting, Gandhi became acquainted with all Indians in Pretoria. Thus, his stay there enabled him to study the social, economic and political conditions of the Indians in the area and such awareness was of invaluable service to him in the future.

While in Pretoria, Gandhi also came in contact with some Christians and he also read books on Christianity and Islam. Tolstoy's book *'The Kingdom of God is within'* greatly impressed him. He also read books on Hinduism sent to him by Raichandbhai from Bombay. All these contacts and readings of books, awakened in him the religious quest which influenced his later life.

Gandhi had come to South Africa to attend the case of Abdulla Sheth. It was no small case and involved a big amount of Rs. 40,000 and was full of intricacies of accounts. Gandhi took the keenest interest in the case and his client reposed full confidence in him. He read all the connected papers and acquired full grasp of the facts of the case. He realized that if the litigation persisted, it would run both the parties of the case who incidentally were relatives and belonged to the same city.

Gandhi apprised both parties of the grave danger in continuing the litigation process which might go on indefinitely to the disadvantage of both parties. He, therefore, got the case resolved through negotiation and a compromise formula to the satisfaction of both parties. Thus, both parties were happy as a result of this solution and Gandhi's joy was boundless. He also realized that the true function of a lawyer was to unite opposing parties. As a result of lesson learnt out of the success of this case, Gandhi in his later life of practicing law, brought about hundreds of compromises.

A year's stay in Pretoria was a most valuable experience in Gandhi's life, about the hard conditions of Indians in South Africa. It was here that he had opportunities of public service and developed some capacity and experience in learning and doing it. He also acquired true knowledge of legal service and also realized the religious spirit as a living force within him.

After concluding the case in Pretoria, Gandhi went back to Durban and began preparing for return to India. However, destiny had something else in store for him. In the farewell party arranged for him by Abdulla Sheth, the gathering prevailed upon him to stay on to fight for the rights of Indian settlers.

This became necessary for him because at that time, the local government was planning to deprive the Indians of their right to elect members of the Natal Legislative Assembly. A bill, to this effect was pending before the Assembly. As Gandhi became aware of it, he realised that if that bill became law, then lots of Indians living will become extremely difficult.

He, therefore, decided to stay back. However, in spite of his persistent campaigns, hard work and publicity, the bill was passed. But Gandhi's efforts brought an awakening in the minds of Indians to fight for their rights. It also acquainted the Indian public back home, for the first time, about the conditions in Natal.

Beside publicity, Gandhi earned love and enthusiasm of Indians in South Africa.

After staying back in Natal, Gandhi applied for admission as an advocate of the Supreme Court. Despite opposition from the local law society, he was enrolled as an advocate. This opposition gave him more publicity and most of the newspapers condemned the opposition.

In order to justify his stay in Natal, Gandhi thought it is necessary to concentrate more on public service. Fc. this purpose, he found the 'NATAL INDIAN CONGRESS,' a public organization, to carry the work forward. Its formation resulted in Indians in South Africa having a common forum. He also took up the cause of indentured Indians and brought them relief from heavy taxation.

During three years stay in South Africa, Gandhi had established a fairly good practice and the people gave him their love and regard. They also felt the need of his presence and assistance. He also found himself entirely absorbed in the service of the community. But, he was away from his family for a long time. So he decided to go to India, bring his wife and children and then settle in South Africa.

While in India, Gandhi meet a number of high dignitaries and acquainted them with the plight of Indians in South Africa. Further, he espoused their cause and elicited sympathy and support through pamphlets, press and public meetings.

On his return voyage, Gandhi was accompanied by his wife and children. The ship cast anchor in the port of Durban but was ordered to put in quarantine. The order of quarantines had more then merely health reasons. The real object of this order was to force the passengers to return to India, as the white settlers had been agitating for the repatriation of Indians from there, to their homeland. Even threats were given to push the passangers into the sea, if they did not agree to go back. Gandhi constantly cheered his fellow passengers and also encouraged them to face the crisis with patience and courage.

Consequently, the passenger and Gandhi were detrain to stay back and not to get cowed down by the threats. They insisted on their right to land at port Natal and finally they got it. The ship was permitted to enter the harbor and the passengers were allowed to land.

On landing at port Natal, Gandhi became the main target of the anger of the white agitators. A group of unruly youngsters who recognized him shouted 'Gandhi!! Gandhi!!'and they were soon joined by others. They attacked him with stones, rotten eggs and his turban was also snatched away. Gandhi was battered and fainted but he was saved by a brave white lady, who was the wife of the superintendent of Police and she knew him and was passing by. She stood between the crowd and Gandhi, and protected him with her parasol. Hence, Gandhi was saved from any further harm. Meanwhile, police reached the spot and he was escorted to a safe place.

Mr. Chamberlain, the then Secretary of State for Colonies, asked the Natal government to prosecute assailants of Gandhi. The representative of Natal government expressed regret over the incident and offered to arrest and prosecute the attackers on identification but Gandhi did not like to prosecute any one.

The attack on Gandhi was condemned by the local press and his refusal to prosecute the assailants was greatly afforested. The attack on Gandhi proved to be a blessing in disguise as it enhanced the prestige of Gandhi and the Indian community in South Africa and made his work easier. This incident also increased his professional practice.

While Gandhi's professional work progressed, he did not feel fully satisfied. He wanted to do some humanitarian work of service. He, therefore, found sometime to do service in a charitable hospital. His work helped patients in the removal of their complaints. This gave him peace and brought close to the suffering of the Indians. This experience prove useful later during the 'Boer war' where he offered nursing services for the sick and wounded soldiers.

Gandhi had two sons in South Africa and his experience in the hospital was also useful in the upbringing of these children.

It was in South Africa that Gandhi came to realize the importance of brahmacharya. He did not desire more children and therefore, began to strive for self-control but this was very difficult. He started to sleep in a separate bed but he was not very successful in achieving his aim. The final resolution was made in 1906, at the time of ZULU 'rebellion', when he offered his services to the Natal government. He then realized that if he wanted to devote himself to the community service then he had to live the life of a 'Vanaprasthi'-who had relinquished the household. After mature thought, he took the path of brahmacharya, in 1906, after consulting his wife who had no objections. Thereafter, he started living a simple life with control of the senses for which he had to make the highest effort.

During the Boer tour in South Africa, though his personal sympathies were with the Boers, he participated with the British to show his loyalty to the British Empire. He collected volunteers and formed an ambulance corps of about 1100 strong. The corps rendered good service which was applauded and got good publicity for the Indians whose prestige was enhanced. The Indian community became more established and Gandhi got into greater touch with indentured Indians. All Indians in South Africa became more united and they also believed that their grievances would be redressed.

The corps was disbanded after six week's service and Gandhi was free from war duty. Gandhi then felt that he was needed more in India than in South Africa. He, therefore, sought permission of his co-workers to return to India. His request was accepted on the condition that he would return to South Africa if the community needed him.

The farewell was over-whelming and he was showered with costly gifts including articles in gold and silver. As Gandhi did not want to keep these gifts, he decided to create a trust for them in favour of the community. Gandhi returned to India in 1901.

After travels to various places, making with high percentage of that time and deliberations with the congress he decided to settle in Bombay. He prospered in his profession. Just then, he received an unexpected summon to return to South Africa in view of the visit of Mr. Chamberlain, the then Secretary of State for the Colonies. He remembered his promise and returned to South Africa again.

As the book is not intended to be another biography of Gandhi, the description of all activities of Gandhi, in detail, while in South Africa, is beyond the scope of this small book. In the next chapter, we shall concentrate on his major experiences and experiments during his entire stay in South Africa.

Experiences in South Africa

Gandhi had gone to South Africa for better financial prospects. There was also a tempting opportunity to see a new country and to have new experiences. Initially, the proposed period of stay of his first visit was not more than a year, but later due to his serious and useful community involvements, his stay was extended for over three years. He arrived in Natal, then proceeded to Pretoria and thereafter, settled in NATAL.

On his first visit, Gandhi sailed for South Africa in April, 1893, and after stay of over three years, returned to India, in the middle of 1896. However, in response to an urgent call he again returned to South Africa in December, 1896. He again visited India in 1901 and attended the Indian National Congress but after a short stay, returned to South Africa towards by the end of 1901. Thereafter, he stayed and worked in South Africa till 1914, after which he finally returned to India in January, 1915, to stay and serve the mother land.

Gandhi stayed in South Africa for about twenty years. This long stay of his life, when he was very young, active and full of ambition to do public work, was full of events and activities, which played a great role in the formation of his character and destiny. In his own words, Gandhi wrote as follows:

"I had gone to South Africa for travel, for finding an escape from Kathiawar intrigues and for gaining livelihood. But as I have said, I found myself in search of God and striving for self-realization."

The description of the details of events and activities of Gandhi Ji in South Africa, is not within the scope of this small book. The intention is to highlight most of the powerful experiences which he had during his stay in South Africa and which greatly influenced his philosophy and actions. We shall make an attempt to describe these experiences and influences under small headings in order to drive home the significance to the general reader.

Escape From Sin During First Voyage

On his first voyage to South Africa in April, 1983, Gandhi and the captain of the ship became great friends. He used to play chess with him and also shared the extra berth in his cabin. At Cinnabar, where the ship halted for more than a week, the captain took Gandhi on an outing where he was pushed into the room of a Negro woman. Gandhi simply stood there dumb with shame. However he came out, unseated without committing any sin. He felt horrified and had a deep sense of shame but thanked God for the narrow escape. This was the third trial of this nature in his life and every time he was saved from sin by the grace of God.

The above incident increased Gandhi's faith in God.

Deplorable Conditions Of Indians In South Africa

As the ship reached Durban, Gandhi watched the people coming on board to meet their friends. He also noticed some sort of snobbishness on the part of those who knew Abdulla Sheth, Gandhi's host. As a result of his keen and quick observations, Gandhi felt that there was not much respect for Indians in South Africa and this really stung him. After a short stay, he found that Indians there were divided into several groups and the majority of Indians belonged to the labouring class. Most Indians were held in contempt and were called as 'COOLIES'. When Gandhi was taken to see the Durban Court, he was asked to remove his turban, which he refused and came out of the court.

While travelling in train in a first class compartment he was thrown out of the train because he was 'colour'. He encountered more hardships and faced indignities while travelling in a stage-coach.

He was even denied room in a hotel. Besides his personal bad experiences due to racial discrimination he also came to know about the several stories of hardships suffered by Indians in South Africa. The Indians, in general, were treated with contempt and the whites wanted them more than the native Negroes, partly because they were coloured and also because, being industrious, they offered competition in agriculture and trade. It was in South Africa that Gandhi learnt about the endless disabilities, hardships and humiliations suffered by the Indians. He also had personal experience of these miseries.

A year's stay in Pretoria was a most valuable experience in his life about the hard conditions of Indians in South Africa. He had opportunities of public service and developed some capacity and experience in learning and doing it.

He also acquired true knowledge of legal service and realized the religious spirit as a living force within him. He also realized that true role of a lawyer was to unite opposite parties to the extent possible.

Gandhi stayed in South Africa for 20 years during which he got to know the people and they also got to know him. He established a fairly good legal practice and people felt the need of his presence and assistance. He also found himself entirely absorbed in the service of the community. As his professional work progressed, he also found sometime for some humanitarian work. He, therefore, started doing service in a small hospital where he helped patients in the removal of their complaints and it brought him close to the suffering humanity. This experience also helped him later in the Boer War, when he offered his services for nursing the sick and the wounded soldiers.

On his second trip to South Africa, Gandhi was accompanied by his wife and two children. Two more children were born in South Africa. Gandhi studied some book on the nursing and rearing of children and this stood him in good stead at the time of the birth of his last child. He himself acted as midwife who was not readily available and helped in the safe delivering of the baby.

With the passage of time, Gandhi got himself involved deeply in the service of the community. At the time of the Zulu 'rebellion' in Natal, Gandhi offered his services to the Natal government. Accordingly, he gave up his house in order to lead the Indian ambulance corps formed by him to help the Natal forces. It was during the difficult time that he thought of requiting the life of household cares, in order to devote himself to the service of the community. He strongly felt that the services for children and wealth was not consistent with the spirit of public service. It was at the slug that he began seriously to think about 'Brahmacharya'.

Vow Of Brahmacharya

It was in South Africa, that after full discussion and mature thought, Gandhi took the vow in 1906. He consulted kasturba who had no objection. It was a difficult decision but he kept his resolve with faith in the sustaining power of God.

He remained celibate from 1906, until his death in 1948. He was 36 when he took the vow. Gandhi believed that his vow of brahmacharya was in response to the demands of public service which called for self-control, chastity of the body and the purity of the mind. The observance of brahmacharya guided him to lead a simple life and he cut down lot of unnecessary household expenditure.

He also believed that his vow would generate tremendous falsely energy for carrying on his strenuous struggle against racial discrimination and other ills of community life. For Gandhi, to achieve perfect brahmacharya, was the highest goal and he made the highest effort to achieve it. His stay in South Africa and the role he played to perform selfless public service greatly encouraged him to achieve this goal.

Birth Of Satyagraha

For Gandhi, the vow of brahmacharya was a great shield against temptation. The observance of brahmacharya slowly led to the foundation of satyagraha, as though he had been preparing him for it. He did not have a preconceived plan for satyagraha, it came rather spontaneously. Gandhi used satyagraha as a technique for fighting injustice and oppression of the white people against the coloured. This was based upon truth and non-violance and proved to be a powerful weapon which was not designed to cause suffering to the opponent but instead resulted in self-suffering in order to make the opponent realize the folly of his mistake.

For Gandhi, satyagraha was a peaceful means to wean away the opponent from error by patience and sympathy. He used this peaceful weapon with great success to restore self-respect, dignity and legal rights of the crowned people in South Africa. It should be noted that the thought of using satyagraha for fighting injustice and oppression, came to Gandhi after seeing the circumstances prevailing in South Africa. The exercise and implementation of this thought into successful action made a great contribution to the making of the Mahatma.

Comparative Study Of Religions

When Gandhi went to South Africa, he had not read much about religion, not even his own religion, Hinduism. In South Africa, as he became entirely absorbed in the service of the community, he made the religion of service as his own. He had great desire for self-realization and believed that this aim could be achieved only through the service.

While in South Africa, Gandhi studied several books on different religions. This study stimulated self-introspection and he also developed the habit of practicing what appealed to him in his studies. He also made an intensive study of Tolstoy's books which made a deep impression on him. He also communicated with his Christian companions, but he could not regard Christianity as the perfect or the greatest religion.

Since his student's days in UK, Gandhi had began a conscious study of different religions. His basic approach was, equal reverence for the best in all religions.

Coping With Shyness

In his childhood, Gandhi was very shy and tried to avoid people's company. His books were his sole companions. The habit of shyness continued even when he went to London for studies. Even during social meetings, he did not have the courage to speak. This shyness he retained throughout his stay in England.

It was only in South Africa that Gandhi got over his shyness, though not completely. He hesitated whenever he had to face strange audience. However, it was in Pretoria, that he made the first public speech in his life, when he called a meeting of all the Indians in Pretoria and shared his thoughts with them. His speech made a considerable impression on the people and he himself felt encouraged. Thereafter, such meetings were held on regular basis and consequently, Gandhi came in contact with all Indians there and also became acquainted with their social, economic and political conditions.

This experience was of invaluable service to him during his later life in South Africa and he also came over his initial shyness.

Spirit Of Service

Gandhi was much devoted to his parents, since his childhood. When his father became bed-ridden, he acted as his nurse. He would give him medicine, dress his wounds and massage his legs. He loved to do this service.

This seed of spirit of service flowered when he settled in South Africa. While his profession progressed, he also felt the urge to do some concrete act of service to his fellow people in South Africa. One day, a leper came to him, and he offered him shelter, dressed his wounds and began to look after him and later he took him to a hospital for proper care. Later, he started doing service in a charitable hospital. During Boer war in South Africa, Gandhi offered his services for nursing the sick and wounded soldiers. He also lent a helping hand to his wife, in bringing up his children. When there was sudden outbreak of plague in the Indian location in Johannesburg, Gandhi nursed the victims day and night and bravely faced the risk of catching the dreaded diseases. Again when the Zulu 'Rebellion' broke out, he offered his services to form an Indian Ambulance corps and served through the war with a corps, of 24 Indian volunteers. During his long stay in South Africa, he rendered selfless service to fight against injustice being inflicted upon the coloured people and to safeguard human rights. In the walk of public service, Gandhi had to undergo lot of hardships, face insults and indignity and was arrested, put in jail several times and this way suffered more hardships. Inspite of there personal afflictions and sacrifices, his spirit of service did not dampen but grew in strength even in the face of more misery and increasing hardships.

Passion For Vegetarianism

Born in VAISHNAV HINDU family, Gandhi and his family were all vegetarians. However, in his school days he started taking meat under the influence of a friend. He discarded this habit soon after, when he realized his folly. Before going to England, he took a vow of not taking meat and he stuck to it thereafter and the passion for vegetarianism, as a mission went on immersing. The seed for vegetarianism was, infact, sown in England, where he started a vegetarian club. In England, he read Salt's book *'Plea for Vegetarianism'* and became vegetarian by choice.

When Gandhi went to South Africa, he made strenuous efforts in this direction. He was always in favour of pure vegetarian diet.

Initially, he thought that since milk is an animal product, it can not be included, strictly speaking in a vegetarian diet. But later, experience tought him that in order to keep perfectly fit, milk should be included in vegetarian diet.

Simple Life

When Gandhi went to England, he tried to become polished and fashionable like an English gentleman. He bought new clothes, got a double watch chain of gold besides a hat and cultivated offer accomplishments in order to fit into a polite society. He also decided to take dancing lessons. But this infatuation for western lifestyle lasted only for a few months and thereafter, he decided to reduce his expenses and concentrated more on a life as a student.

In South Africa too, he started on a life of ease and comfort but this was short lived. When he settled there, he furnished his house with cars but later he began to cut down his expenses. He started to cut his own hair and also learnt washing clothes. He along with his wife, even cleaned chamber pots. In view of increasing household expenses, the tendency towards simplicity began in Durban. As he came under the influence of Ruskin's teachings, his penchant for simpler life grew stronger. The need for furniture in the house and for other physical possessions went on decreasing gradually. The liking for doing all the physical labour personally also increased and this discipline was enforced on family members also. Instead of buying baker's bread, Gandhi started preparing wholemeal bread at home. For this purpose, a hand ground flour mill was purchased. The grinding proved a very useful exercise. As a result of his vow of brahmacharya, he cut down on his food intake, as well. He began to take an exclusive fruit diet and to fast on certain days. As he got accustomed to fasting, he attached greater importance to it and started having only one meal a day on holidays. He also stopped taking tea and finished his last meal before sunset. On one occasion, he gave up salt altogether and continued this restriction for an unbroken period of ten years.

Experiments In Nature Cure Methods

While at Johannesburg, Gandhi used to suffer from frequent headaches and constipation. However, he kept himself going by taking some laxatives and a regulated diet. But he did not feel healthy. Meanwhile, he read about the benefits of 'No Breakfast' plan and he tried it on himself. This brought improvement and he concluded that he was eating more than was necessary. Earlier, he was never a spare eater and enjoyed three square meals and afternoon tea. As a result of less eating, his headache entirely disappeared.

For constipation, he tried hot bath and earth treatment which consisted in applying to the abdomen moistened cleaned earth poultice. This natural treatment cured him of constipation. Gandhi believed that there was little need for drugs, if one takes well-regulated diet and try nature cure methods and other household remedies. One should not become slave of the body but should remain its master and practice self-control and restraint in conduct and diet.

Experience In Legal Practice

In the practice of his profession as a lawyer in South Africa, Gandhi adopted a simple humanitarian and straight forward approach. As a student, he had heard that 'the lawyer's profession was a liar's profession' but that saying did not influence him. He had no intention of earning either fame, position or money by lying. This principle was put to test in South Africa, but he never resorted to falsehood and a large part of his practice was in the interest of public service.

His charges were nothing beyond his out-of-pocket expense and in some cases, even these he met himself. During his legal practice, he never concealed his ignorance from his clients or his colleagues. He never encouraged his client or his witness to lie, even by doing so he could win the cases. He would always warn his client, at the outset, that he should not expect him to take up a false case. Consequently, he built up such a reputation that no false case used to come to him. The object of his legal practice in South Africa was in the nature of the public service.

The experiences of Gandhi in South Africa in the young formative years spread over long span of twenty years, had a tremendous impact on the building of his character and in the shaping of his multi-dimensional personality. During his stay there, he became acquainted with the miserable conditions of Indian settlers and the unjust and discriminatory treatment of white rulers. He wholly devoted himself in public service and conducted his experiments in truth, non-violence, satyagraha, brahmacharya, self-help and nature cure methods, charity public welfare, fight against social discrimination and much more. As a result of these experience and experiments, when he finally returned to India, he was a mature person, a respected leader and well-established in moral principles. The turning point in his life came about in South Africa. The seeds of his strong moral, non-violent and truthful background were sown in the difficult terrain of discriminatory environment in South Africa. Consequently, when he finally returned to India he was well on the way to being a Mahatma.

Turning Point in the Life of Gandhi

The incident which gave a new direction and resolve and may well be deemed as a 'Turning Point' in his life occurred in South Africa.

A few days after his arrival in Durban, he was travelling in a train to Pretoria. He was travelling in a first class compartment, on a first class seat already booked for him. The train reached Maritzburg, the capital of Natal, at night. A railway servant came and asked him if he needed a bedding. Gandhi said 'No' and he went away. Then a white passenger came, looked at Gandhi and the sight of a coloured man quite disturbed him. He went out and came in again with two officials but they kept quiet. Then another official came and asked Gandhi to move to the van compartment.

Gandhi said 'I have a first class ticket'. The official said 'That does not matter. You must go to the van compartment.'

Gandhi replied 'I was permitted to travel in this compartment at Durban and I insist on going on it'. The official replied 'No, you won't. You must leave this compartment or else I shall have to call a police constable to push you out.'

At this Gandhi said 'Yes, you may. I refuse to get out of my own.'

Then the police constable came. He took Gandhi by hand and pushed him out. The baggage was also taken out. Gandhi refused to go to the van compartment and the train steamed away. He went to the waiting room and sat in with his hand bag leaving the luggage where it was. The railway authorities took charge of the luggage.

Maritzburg being at a high altitude, the cold was extremely bitter. There was no light in the room and Gandhi was without his over coat which was in the luggage. He did not dare to ask for it lest he should be insulted again. So, he sat in the dark room and shivered without any companion. This was a critical juncture for Gandhi who began to think of what to do?

Should he fight against injustice or go back to India or should he go on to Pretoria for the job and return to India after finishing the case in hand? He thought it would be cowardice to return to India without doing his duty. Inspite of the hardships and the insults, he decided to stay and fight against the disease of colour prejudice so he took the next available train to Pretoria.

Gandhi Ji has mentioned this incident in his autobiography that took place during a train journey in South Africa when he was humiliated, assaulted and pushed out of the train on a severely cold night. His fault was that he was a coloured man.

This incident deepened his feeling for the coloured people and he resolved to fight against the injustice, coloured prejudice and the discriminatory treatment being meted out to the Indian setllers in South Africa. This was a momentous decision and a turning point in the life of Gandhi Ji. Had he turned back to India, the story of his life would have been different altogether!

At the same railway station, hundred years later, a grandson of Gandhi Ji received the conferment of 'FREEDOM OF THE CITY' of Maritzburg on Mahatma Gandhi by the former President of South Africa-Nelson Mandela.

This was a great tribute to the memory of Mahatma Gandhi.

Some Powerful Influences on Gandhi

Some individuals, incidents and learning experience leave powerful influences in the life of a person and Gandhi was no exception. Some powerful influences which had great impact on the life of Gandhi Ji are briefly described below.

His Parents

Gandhi was the youngest child in the family. His mother was deeply religious, gentle, devout and strict in her observance of rituals of fast and prayer. She was very strict in keeping her vows and would not take her meals without saying daily prayers. She was very truthful. In his later days, Gandhi too exhibited most of these tendencies which he inherited from his mother. His mother was more religious than her husband and Gandhi inherited purity more from his mother than father.

In his own words, Gandhi said "The outstanding impression my mother has left on my memory, is that of saintliness."

Gandhi's father was truthful, brave, generous, but short-tempered and to some extent, he might have been even given to carnal pleasures for fourth time when he was over forty. But he was incorruptible, truthful and was widely respected.

These special tendencies of his parents, both positive and negative must have influenced Gandhi to a great extent. He became a votary of TRUTH which he equated with GOD. He was tender loving, pure-hearted and deeply religious in the true sense.

He had the carnal desire in his early life but completely overpowered this negative tendency as he grew up in his life.

Mahatma Gandhi's parents

Thus, parental influences played a great role in shaping Gandhi's life.

Some Foreign Influences

Gandhi was influenced by Thoreau, who taught him through his essay on *'Duty of Civil Disobedience'*, scientific confirmation of what he practiced in South Africa.

Great Britain gave him Ruskin whose book *'Unto this Last'* transformed him overnight. This was the first book of Ruskin which Gandhi read while travelling in a train in South Africa. During the days of education, he had read practically nothing besides text books. This book of Ruskin exerted an instantaneous influence on Gandhi. He later on translated it into Gujarati under the title *'Sarvodaya'* which means the welfare of all. He found some of his deepest convictions reflected in this great book.

Russia gave Gandhi Tolstoy, a teacher who furnished a reasoned basis for the practice of creed of non-violence. Tolstoy blessed his movement in South Africa. In his letter to Gandhi, Tolstoy made a prophecy that the movement lead by the former would bring a message of hope to the down trodden people of the earth.

It was in England that he read Salt's *'Plea for Vegetarianism'* and was much impressed by it. He read this book from cover to cover and from the date of its reading became a vegetarian by choice. He not only made his choice, but also made it a mission to spread vegetarianism, and also started a vegetarian club for this purpose.

It was during his stay in UK that Gandhi read *'The Light of Asia'* by Sir Edwin Arnold and also his *'The Song Celestial'*, besides *'Key to Theosophy'* and *'The New Testament'*. All these books stimulated him to read more about spirituality. He was greatly impressed by the *'Sermon on the Mount'* which he compared with the *Gita*.

Influence Of Religion

Gandhi was a deeply religious person. But his concept of religion was very broad based and all pervasive. We have separately described, briefly, his views on religion which exerted great influence on him, his life and all activities.

In his own words, 'I could not live for a single second without religion. My politics and all other activities are derived from my religion.'

For him, religion means being bound to GOD who rules your every breath. His religion was a rational and ethical one. For him, no religion was higher than truth and righteousness and true religion and morality are inseparable. His belief in God and in fundamental truths of all great religions made him a crusader of the cult of religious harmony, love and universal brotherhood. For him, even the tiniest activity was governed by religion. His practice of non-violence, love, truth and other moral values whether in politics or other aspects of his life were inspired by his concept of true religion. That renunciation as the highest form of religion, appealed to him greatly.

An Unfriendly Influence

While at school, Gandhi had very few friends, but there were two who might be called as intimates. However, one of these friendships, he regarded as a tragedy of his life as it had a very bad influence on him in his early life.

This friend was bold, athletic and had a good physique and would greaty impress Gandhi with his physical exploits which the latter lacked. Gandhi was dazzled by his physical powers and desired to be like him, as he was timid and fearful of thieves, ghosts and serpents etc. He was afraid of darkness and would not dare to go out at night. Knowing Gandhi's weakness, his friend would tell him that meat eating will make him brave, daring and unafraid of thieves and ghosts etc. Under his influence, Gandhi took to meat eating. The same friend once took Gandhi to a brothel. Everything was pre-arranged and even the bill had been paid.

But with God's grace, Gandhi was saved from committing any sin. There were four more similar incidents but due to good fortune, he was saved each time. Gandhi called there moral lapses as the carnal desire was there even though no sin was committed physically. Later on, Gandhi reflected upon there evil vendencies and moral deficiencies and overpowered there negative influences and freed himself from the bad influence of his friend. Consequently, he gave up meat eating for good.

Play Of Raja Harishchandra

Two religious stories deeply influenced Gandhi. One was the story of Raja Harishchandra.

In his childhood, Ghandhi saw a performance by a travelling dramatic company. This religious story narrated the pathetic story of suffering of an ancient king who sacrificed everything including his kingdom and family for the sake of truth. The story goes like this.

Thousand years ago, there was a king who was very truthful, honest and generous. Once a great famine befell his land and the kind hearted king donated all that he possessed to help the poor. One of the gods disguised himself as a beggar, came to the king and asked for alms. The king gave him all that he had but the holy man was not satisfied. So the king became the servant of an untouchable (DOM) in order to meet the demands of the holy man. The holy man then went away. The DOM assigned the job of collecting fees from those who came to burn their dead at the cremenation point.

Meanwhile, king's only son died and the queen carried the corpse to the burning ghat. King Harishchandra demanded the fee but the poor lady had no money. She pleaded with her husband, saying 'All that I have is this sari which I am wearing'. But the king wanted to perform his duty. So the queen offered to part with her sari in payment of the fee.

As she started removing her sari, the gods were shaken and came down to earth and revived the young prince to life. They admired the courage, devotion to duty and truthfullness of the king and the queen and took them into heaven.

This play influenced Ghandhi greatly and he wanted to act himself like Harishchandra. The great idea of TRUTH was thus implanted in him in early childhood and it grew naturally to full bloom in later life. Truth became God for him.

Story Of Shravan Kumar

The other story which influenced him and taught him to serve his fellow men was the story of Shravan Kumar.

While in primary school, Ghandhi read that the parents of Shravan Kumar were blind and he carried them in a sling an his shoulder from one place of pilgrimage to another. He would work for the whole day to earn a living and serve his parents in every way to make their life comfortable. He was the only support of his blind parents who were entirely dependant on him.

One day, Shravan had gone to the stream to fetch water for his parents. King Dashrath was also hunting in nearly forest. He mistook Shravan for a deer and let fly an arrow which killed Shravan, while he was drawing water in his pitcher to quench the thirst of his parents. This scene was depicted in a picture which greatly moved Gandhi. Shravan was mortally wounded and cried in pain. Even then he asked king Dashrath to carry water to his parents and quench their thirst. King did so and there after broke the news of the death of their son and expressed his sorrow. The old parents could not bear the loss of their son and they died.

This story had great influence on Gandhi who took great pleasure in serving his parents. In his later life, he gave up all his comfort and possessions in order to serve the poor, the community and the country.

Harishchandra and Shravan Kumar became his heroes.

The Influence Of The Gita

The teaching of the GITA had a profound influence on Gandhi Ji. In his own words, he writes as follows-

"The GITA is the universal mother. I find a solace in the Gita which I miss even in the 'Sermon on the Mount'. When disappointment stores me in the face and all alone, I see not one ray of light, I go back to the Gita. I find a verse here and a verse there and immediately begin to smile in the midst of over whelming tragedies."

The above lines indicate how greatly Gandhi was influenced by the Gita. However, strange as it may look, it was in UK that he was introduced to the Gita when he came across two Theosophists who talked to him on this subject. Till then, he had not read the great book. It was then that he became more acquainted with it by reading sir Edwin Arnold's translation *'The Song Celestial'*. Thereafter, he read almost all the English translations of it and regarded sir Edwin Arnold's translation as the best. Later in life, the Gita became a book of his daily reading.

The teaching of the Gita left a deep impression on the mind of Gandhi. These impressions grew deeper with the passage of time and he regarded it as the book par excellence for the knowledge of truth.

Some Other Influences

Apart from the major influences on Gandhi mentioned earlier, he was deeply impressed by some other individuals who inter-alia include Raichandbhai, sir Pherozeshah Mehta, Lokmanya Tilak and G.K.Gokhale.

Raichandbhai though a business man, was a real seeker after truth. He was absorbed in godly pursuits in the midst of business.

Gandhi enjoyed the closest association with him and got his help and guidance on many occasions. About him, Gandhi once said "no on else has ever made on me the impression that Raichandbhai did, whose words went straight home to him and his intellect and moral earnestness left deep impression on me." Under his influence Gandhi read Upanishads and some other Hindu religious books. As stated by Gandhi, three moderns left a deep impress on his life and captivated him. Raichandbhai by his living contact, Tolstoy by his book, *'The kingdom of God is within you'* and Ruskin by his book *'Unto This Last'*.

Sir Pherozeshah Mehta seemed to Gandhi like the Himalaya, the Lokmanya like the ocean and Gokhale was like the Glances. In the sphere of politics, Gokhale occupied a unique place in the least and life of Gandhi, who referred to Gokhale as his spiritual Guru and his master in matters of public work. Gandhi had a long and useful association with Gokhale.

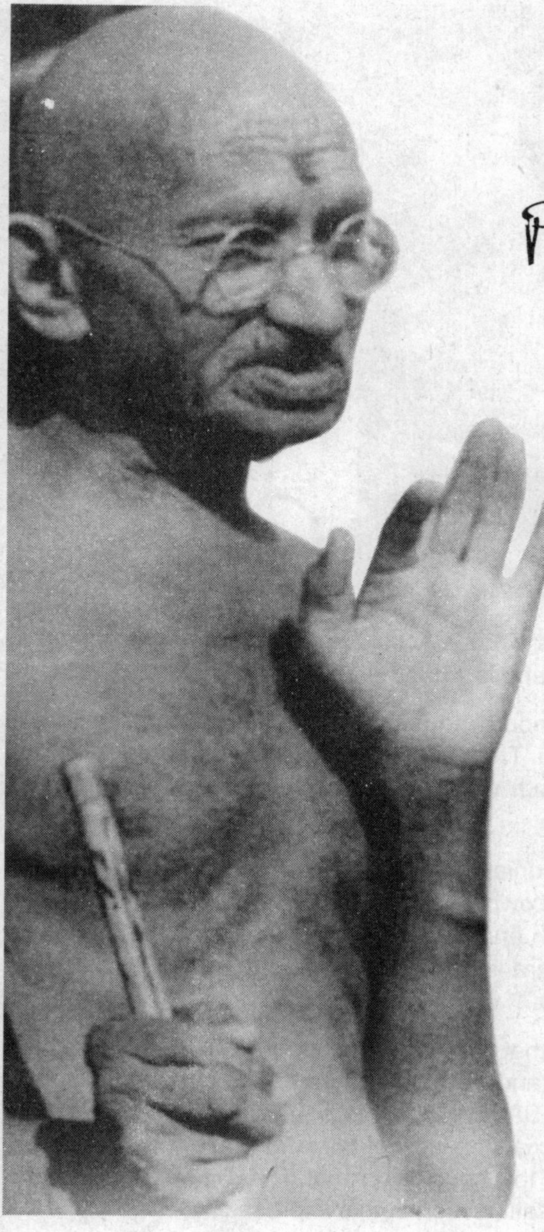

Part - 2

- Truth, Love and Non-violence
- Non-violence
- Satyagraha
- Sarvodya
- Brahmacharya
- Views on God
- Views on Religion
- Aesthetics of Gandhi
- Manual Labour and Gandhi
- Miscellaneous thoughts of Gandhi

Truth, Love and Non-Violence

"The way to truth lies through ahimsa (Non-violence)."

M.K. Gandhi

Gandhi Ji declared 'I am devoted to none but truth' and 'truth is the first thing to be sought for'. What is Truth? According to him, "Truth resides in every human heart and is what the voice within tells you."

Gandhi Ji had an underlying faith in God translated as Truth. He adopted the formula 'Truth is God'. He believed that there is only one fundamental truth which is Truth itself, otherwise known as Non-violence.

The edifice of Gandhian philosophy had two pillars. Truth and Non-violence. In his own words he said, "I would not sacrifice two things, namely, truth and non-violence, for all the world. For me, truth is God and there is no way to find Truth except through the way of non-violence."

Gandhi Ji argued that in Hindu philosophy, God alone is and nothing else exists and the same thought is expressed in Islam. The Sanskrit word SATYA which is equivalent of Truth, literally means that which exists. In view of this and similar other reasons, Gandhi Ji came to the conclusion that TRUTH is GOD and he found the greatest satisfaction in this expression.

Gandhi Ji believed that truth is the first thing to be sought for and beauty and goodness will then be added into you. Throughout his life, Gandhi Ji was a seeker of Truth and he was always making a ceaseless efforts to find it. There was no room for untruth in his writings which were free from hatred. He believed that it is love that sustains the earth and there only is life where there is love. He felt that love and truth are too sides of the same coin and the whole world could be conquered by truth and love. In the English language, love has many meanings. For Gandhi Ji, love in the sense of passion was something degrading. He found that love in the sense of AHIMSA (non-violence) was more appropriate meaning. Believing TRUTH is GOD, and if you want to seek Truth as God, then the only inevitable means is love which is non-violence.

Gandhi Ji called himself a humble and earnest seeker of Truth. In his search, he found beauty in truth or through it. He believed that there is no beauty apart from truth although truth may sometimes manifest itself in forms which may not be beautiful outwardly.

He quoted the example of Socrates who was the most truthful man of his time and yet he is said to have the ugliest facial features in Greece.

According to Gandhi Ji, truth resides in every human heart and one has to search for it there and to be guided by truth as one sees it. He was devoted to none but truth and made ceaseless efforts to find it. The way to find truth is to realize oneself, in other words to attain spiritual perfection. The mission of life should be to strive after perfection which is self-realization. The path to it is straight but narrow and it is like the edge of a sword but one who strives, never perishes. A life of perfect continence in thought, speech and action is necessary for attaining success in this path. Gandhi Ji claimed to have come nearer to God and Truth, after sixty years of striving.

Gandhi Ji's perception of truth was not different from GOD. That is why he would say 'Truth is GOD'. After his continuous and relentless search about truth, he came to the conclusion that the nearest approach to truth was through love. The definition 'Truth is God' gave him the greatest satisfaction and to find truth as God, the only means is love, that is, non-violence. As he believed that ultimately the means and ends are convertible, he also agreed with those who say 'God is Love'. Gandhi Ji also believed that truth and love are two sides of the same coin. Then God, truth, love and non-violence have similar connotations. In his own words, Gandhi Ji said "I would not sacrifice truth and non-violence for all the world. For me Truth is God and there is no way to find Truth except the way of non-violence." He also said "I have nothing new to teach the world. Truth and non-violence are as old as the hills."

Non-violence

According to Gandhi Ji, non-violence is the greatest force at the disposal of mankind. It is a power which can be enjoyed all children, young men and women or grown up people provided they have faith in God and have equal love for all mankind. It has to be accepted as the law of life as a whole and not be applied to isolated acts only. The principle of non-violence enjoins complete abstention of exploitation in any form.

Gandhi Ji used the word AHIMSA for non-violence which in its positive form, means the largest love. A true follower of ahimsa must love even his enemy. In actual practice, ahimsa must include truth and fearlessness. A man can not practice ahimsa without courage and fearlessness. Non-violence is not a resignation from fighting against wickedness.

For Gandhi Ji, non-violence was not a mere philosophical principle. It was the rule and breath of his life, a matter of heart and not of intellect. It is the highest duty according to the scriptures.

Gandhi believed that the first condition of non-vionence is justice all round in all walks of life. It may be too much to expect from human nature but Gandhi did not think so. He thought that the follower of non-violence should cultivate the capacity to make sacrifice of the highest type.

Non-violence should also have no cause for fear. It is essential to overcome all fear in order to practice non-violence to perfection. The votary of ahimsa should have only one fear, that is of GOD.

Gandhi felt that there will be violence if we mearly love those who love us. It is non-violence only when we love even those who hate us. It is very difficult to love the hater but all great and good things are difficult. But, it would become possible to do so if we have the grace of God and the will to do it.

According to Gandhi Ji, history tells us that man has been steadily progressing towards ahimsa. In far remote time, men were cannibals. Then they gave it up and became hunters of animal. Then they took to agriculture. Gradually, they settled to some stable, civilized life form of nomads and founded settlements, villages and towns. From individual he progressed to a member of a family, of a community and of a nation. All these are signs of progressive ahimsa.

Gandhi Ji commended the example Ahimsa, more or less of avatars and prophets who tought the lesson. He thought man as animal is violent, but as spirit is non-violent. He ceases to be non-violent, the moment he rises to the level of spirit. That is why all holy spiritual persons have tought the lessons of truth, love, justice and brotherhood etc., which are all signs of ahimsa. He further quoted the example of peaceful families and societies which are bound by love and law of non-violence. In his pursuit of Satyagraha, Gandhi did not admit of violence. He adopted passive resistance as a method of securing rights by personal suffering.

Some of Gandhi's companions told him that truth and non-violence had no place in politics and worldly affairs. He did not agree. All through his life, he experimented with their introduction and application in everyday life and found results to his satisfaction. He found non-violent weapons of satyagraha and non-cooperation, a complete substitute of violence and utilized these weapons very effectively.

As a general rule, Gandhi commended non-violence in all departments of life but he also felt that perfect non-violence is impossible so long as we exist physically. In some forms taking life may be a duty. We destroy certain forms of life as much we think necessary, for sustaining our body.

Thus for life, we take food, vegetable and other things. Similarly, we destroy mosquitoes and other harmful insects to safeguard our health. We kill carnivorous beasts, snakes etc. Even man-slaughter may be necessary in some cases. Supposing, a mad man or a criminal or a terrorist is on a killing spree, what will you do? You will have to use violence and kill him. Gandhi recommended even mercy killing to relieve an animal or a man from the agony of an unvaluable pain resulting from a fatal injury or an incurable disease.

He did not think that non-violence is a resignation from all real fighting against wickedness. However, the non-violence of his conception is an active and real fight against evil without the spirit of hatred and retaliation. In doing so, he would prefer the resistance of the soul rather then the physical resistance but such an approach is an ideal state.

According to Gandhi Ji, the positive form of ahimsa involves the highest love, greatest charity. As a follower of ahimsa, he would love his enemy and would apply the same rule to the wrong-doer who is enemy or a stranger as he would to his erring son. A man can not fear or frighten his loved one. The ahimsa in its actual form includes fearlessness and truth. A man can not practice ahmisa and a coward at the same time as its practice demands the greatest courage. Non-violence and cowardice do not go together. His conception of non-violence does not admit of running away from danger. If the choice is between violence and cowardly flight, he would prefer violence to cowardice. In his own words, it was manly enough to defend one's own property, honour, or religion, even at the point of sword. It was manlier and nobler to defend them without seeking to injure the wrong-doer. But it is unmanly and dishonorable to forsake the post of duty, in order to save one's own skin. His creed of violence is an extremely active force which has no scope for cowardice or weakness. In this context, Gandhi had said, 'if we do not know how to defend ourselves, our women and our place of worship by the force of suffering i.e. non-violence, we must be at-least able to defend all these by fighting'. He added that he would risk violence a thousand times then the emasculation of a whole race. He believed that where there is only a choice between cowardice and violence, he would advise violence. He said 'I would rather have INDIA resort to arms in order to defend her honour than that she could in a cowardly manner become or remain a helpless witness to her own dishonour. Non-violence in its dynamic condition means conscious suffering, but not mere submission to the will of the evil doer. It means putting of one's whole world against the will of the tyrant. Working under this law, it was possible to defy the whole might of the British empire and to safeguard the honour of India.

Gandhi firmly believed that non-violence is infinitely superior to violence as forgiveness is more manly than punishment. Non-violence come from the strength of the spirit just as forgiveness is possible from the position of strength as it can not pretend to proceed from a weak and helpless creature.

In common parlance, non-violence means non-killing or non-injuring any living being. Such a meaning makes it negative in character. However, Gandhi enlarged the very meaning of non-violence by giving it larger than life role. In this context, it may be worth while to acquaint the reader with following quotations of Gandhi Ji.

- "In its positive form, ahimsa means the largest love, the greatest charity. If I am a follower of ahimsa. I must love my enemy."
- "Complete non-violence is complete absence of ill-will against all that lives."
- "Non-violence in its active form means goodwill towards all the living."
- "When there is no compassion, there is no non-violence. The test of ahimsa is compassion."
- "Ahimsa is a great force which is active every moment of our lives. It is felt in every action and thought."
- "The acid test of non-violence is that one thinks, speaks and acts non-violently even when there is the greatest provocation to be violent."

- "For me non-violence is not a mere philosophical principle. It is the rule and the breath of my life."
- "Ahimsa is the farthest limit of humility."
- "The only virtue I want to claim is truth and non-violence."
- "Our scriptures declare that there is no dharma higher then truth. But non-violence, they say, is the highest duty."

While talking of applying the principle of non-violence in all walks of life, there is no room for falsehood, fraud, forgery, despite, deception hypocrisy, ill-will, hatred and similar other negative and harmful tendencies and acts like that in our daily life. Gandhi considered all these negative tendencies and acts as different forms and shapes of violence. His principle of non-violence includes the pursuit of truth, righteousness, love, compassion, and good will for all beings, in thought, word and deed.

Gandhi Ji proclaimed that the creed of non-violence is not meant only for richers and saints as it is meant for the common people, as well. The richer and saints who discovered the laws of non-violence in the midst of violence, taught the world that its salvation lay 'not through violence but through non-violence'. Lord Budha, Mahavira, Jesus Christ, Kings Ashoka Socrates, Tolstoy and several other personalities are the brightest examples of exponents of non-violence. In modern times, Gandhi was an ardent practitioner of non-violence. He believed in non-violence, he practiced and preached this doctrine relentlessly throughout his life. He applied this principle with strong conviction not only in his personal life but also in the social and political spheres.

There is no exaggeration in saying that his life, ever since he became a notary of non-violence, was directed and regulated by the principle of non-violence.

He was the greatest champion of non-violence, of his time who lived and died for truth and non-violence.

Satyagraha

In South Africa, Gandhi found himself in an entirely different world. The white settlers there treated the coloured people with contempt. Every Indian, whether he was a businessman or an office-goer was called a 'coolie'. Those who actually worked as labourers were treated worse. No dark persons was allowed to enter a hotel, walk on a pavement along with a white man or travel in the same coach in which a white man was travelling. These were the days in Africa when several laws were being passed against the coloured settlers.

During his stay in South Africa, Gandhi came across several cases of insulting behaviour and maltreatment of Indian settlers at the hands of white people. In some cases, he himself became a victim of such maltreatment and discrimination. There experiences deepened his feelings for the Indian settlers and he made an intimate study of their hard conditions. Greatly touched by their plight and having himself been a victim of colour prejudice and racial discrimination in South Africa, Gandhi initiated and spearheaded a non-violent movement of Indian settlers in Transvaal against the unjust and racially discriminatory rule of the white settlers and government. Gandhi called this movement SATYAGRAHA.

What is Satyagraha?

The term satyagraha is a Sanskrit word and consists of two words, satya and agraha. The meaning of satya is 'truth' while agraha means 'adherence', 'insistence' or 'holding'.

Thus satyagraha implies, adherence to truth or holding on to truth.

Dandi Salt March

During his experiences in the earlier stages, Gandhi discovered that the pursuit of Satyagraha should not admit violence being inflicted on one's opponent who should be persuaded to refrain from wrong doing by patience and sympathy.

As patience involves self-suffering, the doctrine of satyagraha means vindication of truth, not by infliction of suffering on the opponent, but on one's self. This is a method of securing rights by personal suffering and is the reverse of armed resistance. It is admitted that sacrifice of self while fighting against injustice is superior to sacrifice of others.

Gandhi considered that truth and non-violence are two sides of the same coin. He also equated truth with love and morality. In other words, Satyagraha implies an activity or force born out of truth, non-violence and love. Thus, it may be called as truth force, love force or moral force. To quote Gandhi "Satyagraha is a moral weapon to fight untruth with truth and violence with non-violence". A rotary of non-violence will be willing to die himself, so that the others may live. Gandhi called it as 'soul force' which involves self-sacrifice and is superior to 'body force'.

During his more then five decade long social career, Gandhi evolved the method and technique of satyagraha to fight against social and political wrongs. He employed it as a method of peaceful resistance against unjust laws, wrong customs and evil practices. In the application of satyagraha, he formulated certain rules of moral discipline to be adopted by a follower of this path, some of which may be stated, in his own words, as follows:-

- "Try to overcome evil by good, anger by love, untruth by truth and himsa by ahimsa."
- "In satyagraha, there is not the remotest idea of injuring the opponents. It involves the conquest of the adversary by self-suffering."
- "The appeal of satyagraha is to the heart of the wrong-doer. The object is to convert and not to coerce the wrong-doer."
- "A Satyagrahi should avoid violence, abusive language and even ill-will in thought, against the opponent."
- "A Satyagrahi should have inflicting faith in God, truth, love and goodness of human nature."
- "A Satyagrahi should always be ready for an honourable settlement with the opponent."
- "A Satyagrahi should try to understand his opponent's viewpoint."
- "A Satyagrahi should constantly keep watch on his own faults and mistakes and always try to correct himself."
- "He should observe a moral discipline by imbibing and practicing the virtues of purity, self-restraint, patience, self-control, fearlessness, non-stealing, non-possession, celibacy and similar other moral qualities and restraints."

According to Gandhi Ji, there are four basic ideas underlying the spirit of satyagraha as follows:-

1. It is essentially a soul force or love force or truth force.
2. It rejects and excludes the use of violence or physical force.
3. It involves self-suffering and requires the satyagrahi to make an approach to the heart of the opponent or the wrong-doer.
4. It believes in the adoption of pure and good means for achieving pure ends.

Gandhi believed that the method of satyagraha involves persuasive efforts which include discussions, negotiations, persuasions, appeals, meetings, arbitrations etc. If all these methods fail, then the final resort is to appeal to the heart of the opponent by resorting to self-suffering and self-sacrifice.

In the actual application of satyagraha and on the basis of his accumulated experience of several decades, Gandhi has propounded four types of forms or methods of satyagraha, as follows:-

1. **Purificatory Devices** – These include pledges, prayers and fasts. The path of self-purification is hard and steep, it involves self-discipline and self-suffering. Gandhi had several bitter public and private experiences which threw him in temporary despair. He was able to get rid of that despair through prayer. He was a man of power which came from prayer. His pledges, vows and fasts were non-violent means to achieve certain ends. These devices acted in a manner, which approached to the heart in order to bring about desirable changes and results. Gandhi used the mechanism of fasts successfully.

2. **Non-cooperation** – Gandhi was an uncompromising opponent of violent methods even to serve the noblest causes. The method of non-cooperation with the opponent or the unjust system was therefore a potent non-violent weapon, which he used effectively. Various methods of non-cooperation include boycott, strike, resignation, surrender of titles and other privileges accorded by an unjust ruling set-up and so on.

3. **Civil Disobedience** – This method consists of picketing, protest marches, non-payment of unnecessary taxes, defiance of arbitrary and unjust laws which are against the well-being of the people.

4. **Constructive Program** – This is a long drawn socio-economic plan to be followed by a satyagrahi for the whole life. This is based on the actual practice of the principles of truth, love and non-violence.

Gandhi belived that non-cooperation is a universal remedy against social, economic and political evils. He emphasized that a satyagrahi should face hardships and bear sufferings cheerfully while offering non-cooperation with evils of exploitation, violence and oppression. However, if the method of non-cooperation fails then civil-disobedience is inevitable.

Gandhi offered satyagraha in South Africa to fight against discriminatory laws and treatment of white people and also applied the method in the Indian National Movement during the struggle for seeking the freedom of India.

Satyagraha as conceived by Gandhi was learnt in South Africa and was nurtured and flourished in India against the British rule. In the struggle for India's independence, Gandhi insisted upon the adoption of humane methods based on non-violence and self-suffering which formed the core of satyagraha.

To quote Dr. S. Radha Krishnan, "Gandhi was the first in human history to extend the principle of non-violence from the individual to the social and political plane."

Sarvodaya

During a train journey in South Africa, Gandhi Ji read Ruskin's book *'Unto This Last'*. This book caused a magic spell on him and later, he translated it into Gujarati, entitling it *'Sarvodaya'* which means the *'Welfare of all'*.

Gandhi Ji discovered some of his deepest convictions reflected in this book, which transformed his life. The teachings of this book as understood by him are briefly dated as follows:-

1. The good of the individual is contained in the good of all.
2. All have the same right of earning their livelihood from their work.
3. A life of labour is the life worth-living.

Gandhi Ji believed in the greatest good of all as against the doctrine of the greatest good of the greatest number. He called the latter as heartless and a harmful doctrine for the humanity.

He argued that in order to achieve the supposed good of 51 per cent, the interest of 49 per cent may have to he ignored or sacrificed. Thus, the only real, dignified, human doctrine is the greatest good of all which can be achieved through non-violent means.

Gandhi was not a mere mystic but an inversely practical man. He emphasized that the principles which he held true and saved should be applied in practical form through the life of individuals and in the actual working of the society. The constructive work which he had undertaken in his life time, was, therefore, practical application of his fundamental principles of Truth and Non-violence. In the long run, he aimed to help create a society based on these principles.

Gandhi Ji emphasized upon the purity of means inorder to achieve any right goal. He believed 'as the means so the end'. He felt that there is no wall of separation between means and ends. He declared 'ahimsa is the means and truth is the end'. Means and ends were convertible terms in his philosophy of life. In the context, he was an uncompromising opponent of violent means even to serve the noblest cause. He was fully convinced that permanent good can never be the outcome of untruth and violence. He also thought that it was a mistaken belief that there was no connection between the means and the end. He argued that 'you can not get a rose through planting a noxious weed'. According to him, there is the same inviolable connection between the means and the end, as there is between the seed and the tree. Thus impure means result in an impure end. One can not reach truth by untruthfulness and truthful conduct can only reach truth. Therefore, only truthful, non-violent and pure hearted people can establish sarvodaya or good of all.

It is unfortunate that Gandhi's life tree was cut midway and he did not live to see the actual fruition of his ideal of sarvodaya. After his passing away, constructive workers from various parts of the country assembled at Sevagrama and formed a loose sort of organization known as 'sarvodaya samaj'. It is an ideal which is vast in every direction like any ocean. It was not a party or creed or a limited organization. A member (sevak) of the Sarvodaya Samaj is free from all organizational control and there is no external authority over him. He may work at his own place alone or with others as he likes. Whoever believes in the sarvodaya ideal is in it. There is no politics in it. The ideal of sarvodaya echo the thoughts of saint Tulsidas as follows:-

"Generally people desire their personal good. A few desire the good of their own people. But only the servants of god desire the good of everyone."

The ideal of sarvodaya aimed at bringing an ideological revolution which is not the hand made of politics. It is also wrong to think that the social revolution can be achieved through political power. Such a revolution, if brought about, would be of a temporary nature and for a limited number of people. The aim of sarvodaya is mixing ourselves completely with the entire society and give it a shape of the pure spirit free from egotism and make it universal, beyond caste, card, class, colour, country and race. This would correspond with the Vedic concept of 'One World Family'.

In order to give the ideal of sarvodaya, a practiced shape, Sarva-Seva Sangh was formed of which the sarvodaya samaj was a conceptual association of like-minded people. The Sangh was an All India Institution of Planners and Executors of Activities and Work Programmes. It worked as a confederation for tendering advice and help to the workers of the Sarvodaya Samaj. It is an organization for activities and coordination of the work of various set-ups involved in constructive programmes. It worked as a serving institution not connected with any political party.

Vinoba Bhave, the closest disciple of Gandhi Ji, after the latter's death, carried forward the message of sarvodaya. In order to make the meaning and implications of the word 'sarvodaya', he laid down the following two rules:-

1. Have concern for other's needs and do not pursue your own needs in such a way as would harm others;

2. One must earn one's bread by one's own labour without being burden upon others.

He believed that the observance of these rules would pave the path to sarvodaya. He felt that the rules would create happy families and it should not be difficult to extend them to the society at large.

Sarvodaya has been the basic idea of Gandhi Ji's philosophy. It is a sad commentary that it remained only as an ideal in books and after Gandhi's departure was soon forgotten!

Brahmacharya

For Gandhi Ji, brahmacharya was a condition for complete devotion to work. Brahmacharya was therefore considered an important observance for the inmates of his ashram.

What was Gandhi's ideal of brahmacharya?

For him, it is the way of life which leads to BRAHMA or GOD. In his own words, "it includes full control over the process of reproduction. The control must be in thought, word and deed. If the thought is not under control, the other two have no value."

According to Gandhi Ji, a real brahmachari (who practices brahmacharya) loses the distinction between a man and a woman. Brahmacharya involved complete self-control over the sexual urge. Sexual indulgence was considered by him a serious obstacle.

Even married couples in his ashram were expected to avoid sexual indulgence. He believed that brahmacharya is not a virtue that can be cultivated just by outward restraints. A man who runs away from a necessary contact with a woman does not understand the full meaning of brahmacharya. A man who has attained perfect brahmacharya does not stand in need of protecting walls. But an aspirant, a learner needs them like a fruit plant which needs a protective fence around it. A true brahmachari avoids false restraints.

First of all it is essential to know and understand what true brahmaharya is, then to realize its rule and thereafter to practice and cultivate this virtue in thoughts, words and deeds.

True brahmaharya persists under all conditions and in the face of all obstacles and temptations. A brahmachari should remain unaffected by the sight of a beautiful woman. A true aspirant of brahmacharya need not avoid the contact of a woman or run away out of fear. In such a situation, all that he needs to do is to exercise self-control.

Gandhi's view of brahmacharya had a spiritual aspect. He believed that one could overcome all difficulties by invoking spiritual power through purity of mind and complete control of all senses. All power comes from the preservation and sublimation of the energy that is behind the creation of life. This energy or vitality is dissipated by evil thoughts and acts, consciously and even unconsciously. It is therefore, at most essential to keep full control over thought process through will power and grace of God.

He himself conducted experiments to test his self-control, by sleeping in the company of young woman in his ashram. He also believed that a real brahmachari could not even think of sexual pleasure even in his dream. In his view, brahmacharya was a mental state and was not limited to external conditions only.

However, Gandhi did not condemn the sexual urge and thought it a noble and fine thing that was meant only for the process of creation. There was nothing to be ashamed about it. He therefore, did not totally oppose sexual union as it was meant for procreation but not for lust and sensual gratification. Both husband and wife are required to observe self-control in order to preserve their energies. It they realize the importance and implication of self-control, they will not have sexual union simply for their sexual pleasure, but only when they desire issue as a matter of duty.

For the observance of brahmcharya, it is necessary to disapprove of sensual desires as soon as they arise in the mind and try to keep them down. It is the control of the mind which is absolutely essential. However, if the mind vacillates and wallows in thoughts of pleasure which come from sexual indulgence, then it is better to satisfy the hunger of the body as it is better to enjoy through the body than through the thought of it. Gandhi also did not like a married person to observe celibacy if the partner desired sexual act.

Gandhi believed that the real objective of married life was not sexual pleasure. However through sexual union, nature wanted to achieve its objective of procreation. It therefore implies that sexual union should be resorted to mainly for child birth. He opposed indiscriminate use of contraceptive for birth control for which he recommended self-control. He did not agree with the view that the sexual act is a necessary body function or requirement like sleeping and eating. In his view, the act of generation should be controlled for the ordered growth of the world which is the playground of God and should reflect his glory. He who realizes this, will exercise self-control after acquiring knowledge essential for the all round well-being of his progeny.

Gandhi Ji gave valuable hints for the proper observance of brahmacharya for which control of the palate is the first essential. On the basis of his own experience, he found that complete control of the palate made the difficult act of observance of brahmacharya, very easy. His experience taught him that it was wrong to cultivate and continue the relish of tasty food. The cardinal principles in exercising such control is that one should eat not in order to please the palate but to keep the body in good health and going. As he was himself known to observe brahmacharya in thought's, words and deeds, he imposed greater restraints upon himself in the matter of food.

Fasting and restriction in diet played more important role for observance of brahmacharya in his life. He found that passion in man generally co-existed with a hankering after the pleasure of the palate. He, therefore, attached much importance to fasting. However, fasting can help to cruel animal passion only if it is undertaken to observe self-restraint, otherwise it would remain only a futile exercise. Physical fasting will not produce the desired results, if it is not accompanied by mental fasting. More physical fasting may be hypocrisy, and can also be harmful.

As external aids to brahmacharya, fasting, selection and restriction in diet are necessary. The overpowering senses can be kept under control only if they are hedged from all sides. Since they become powerless without food, fasting undertaken with a view to control of the senses is efficacious and helpful. But mechanical fasting is of no avail. Fasting becomes useful when the mind cooperates with the body.

It is unsuited to those who would like to curb their passions. Avoidance of intoxicating drinks and drugs also help in the evolution of the spirit, but it is not an end in itself. Diet is a powerful factor not to be ignored but it is not the whole discipline.

Gandhi Ji declared that one who has attained perfect brahmacharya does not need any protective walls. For him, it is not necessary to run away from contact with a woman. However attractive a woman may be she will not produce any disturbing effect or temptation for him. A true brahmachari does not require any outward restraints since he has created his own natural defences. True brahmacharya persists under all conditions and in the face of all possible temptations.

Gandhi Ji took the vow of brahmacharya in 1906 and he consulted his wife at the time of taking the vow. She had no objection. It was a great and very difficult resolve as the elimination of strange and unusual thing. But he launched forth, with the sustaining power of his full faith in GOD. The vow acted as a sure shield against all temptation and he kept it till the end of his life. Before taking the vow, he was open to temptation, but after it, he was filled with pleasure and wonder of joy, and freedom. It was not an easy thing to keep the vow, but it was a matter of ever increasing joy for him as the time passed on successfully.

According to Gandhi observance of brahmacharya is like walking on the sword's edge and there is need for eternal vigilance every moment. In spite of the task being most difficult and full of temptations, he kept the vow of brahmacharya till death. This was the rarest of rare achievement which exalted him from an ordinary man at birth to the loftiest status of Mahatma.

Views on God

Gandhi Ji believed that there is an indefinable mysterious power that pervades everything. This unseen power itself defies all proof and it can not be perceived through the senses. However, it's possible to reason out it's existence to a limited sense. This is a LIVING POWER that is changeless, formless that creates, dissolves and re-creates. Gandhi believed that this power is Life, Truth, Light, Love and is the supreme GOD. For him, God is not a person but the force.

Gandhi's belief in God is based on faith which transcends reason. He made the world's faith in God as his own and his faith was ineffaceable. God is the essence of all life, is pure and undefiled consciousness. He is eternal. Gandhi considered God as his only guide. He could live without air and water but not without his belief in God. For Gandhi, God is truth and love, fearlessness, ethics and morality, source of light and life and yet above and beyond all these, God is all things to all men.

Gandhi said that it was difficult to define God and there were innumerable definitions of God because his manifestations were innumerable. But Gandhi worshipped God as truth only. He believed that full realization of God is impossible in this embodied life. While we fail to perceive God though the senses, we can feel him if we withdraw ourselves from the senses. The subtle, delicate, divine music of God is always going on within us, but the loud senses drown it and we don't hear it. All that we need is make ourselves fit for the perception. Sense perception can be false and deceptive. When there is realization outside the senses, it is infallible. Such a perception has been achieved by an unbroken line of saints, sages and prophets in all parts of the world, at different times.

Gandhi Ji declared that to seek God, one need not go on a pilgrimage or light lamps before an image or perform similar other rituals. As God resides in our hearts, we need not look for him outside. Personally, Gandhi did not believe in idol worship and an idol did not excite a feeling veneration in him. However, he thought of idol worship. He felt that one thing suits one person and another thing may suit another person. Personally, he preferred the worship of the FORMLESS. Gandhi believed in the absolute ONENESS of God and had the fullest trust in him.

Gandhi defined God in terms of Truth. Although, God can he defined in numerous ways and numerous names can he assigned to him, the formula adopted by Gandhi was 'Truth is God'. For him God and Truth are convertible terms. He based his definition of god, on the meaing of the Sanskrit word 'satya' which means that 'which exists always'. Thus God alone exists and there is nothing else beyond him. This definition of God gave Gandhi, the greatest satisfaction and throughout his life, he remained a ceaseless seeker of truth. In order to find truth, the only inevitable means is love, that is non-violence. Accordingly, he would also agree with those who say 'God is LOVE'. But deep down in his heart, he used to say that though God may be love, God is truth, above all. He also went a step further when he declared that truth is god.

Gandhi Ji believed that the ultimate aim of man is the realization of God and the only way to find God is to see him in his creation and be one with it. This can he done by service of all. Therefore, one must be able to love the meanest of creation, as oneself and this is impossible without self-purification in all walks of life. Gandhi further added that the path of self-purification is not easy as it's hard and steep. For this, one has to become absolutely free of passions in thought, dualities of life - love and hatred, attachment and aversion, likes and dislikes and so on. Gandhi termed it as 'TRIPLE PURITY' for which he strived ceaselessly, throughout his life. The attainment of this objective is harder than any other physical or material objective of the world.

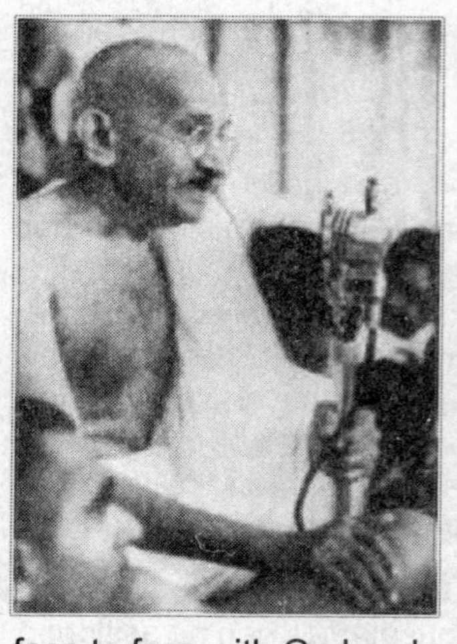

Views on Religion

Gandhi's concept of religion was very broad and all pervasive. By religion, he did not mean a formal or sectarian religion, but that religion which underlies all religion. For him, religion is the path that brings us face to face with God and religion means 'being bound to God'. It is the permanent element in human nature which counts no cost too great in order to find full expression and which leaves the soul restless until it has found itself.

Gandhi believed that religion should pervade all our actions. Here religion does not mean sectarianism. True religion transcends traditional religion like Hinduism, Islam, Christianity etc. It harmonies all religions but does not supersede them to create a new religion. It means a universal belief in orderly moral government of the universe. He thought that various sectarian religions are different roads converging to the same goal and in reality there are as many religions as there are individuals. It does not matter if we take different roads to reach the same point.

Gandhi declared that belief in God is the cornerstone of all religions. In theory since there is one God, there should be only one religion. However, he did not foresee that in actual practice there would be only one religion on earth. Since different people have different conceptions of God based on their different temperaments, traditions, circumstances and environmental conditions. He believed in the fundamental truth of all great religions of the world, which are all God given. He made no distinction between temples, mosques or churches as different places of worship, based on the faith of the respective followers. He also thought that in a sense, there is one fundamental religion in the world. Religion is like one tree with many branches. As branches, one may say, there are many religions but as tree, there is only one religion. He thought that one true and perfect religion becomes many as it passes through the human medium. However, the knowledge of true religion breaks down the barriers between different faiths. After long study and experience of religious thoughts. Gandhi come to the following conclusions:-

1. All religions are true.
2. All religions have some error in them.
3. All religions are almost as dear to me as my own Hinduism, in as much as all human beings should be as close to one as one's own close relatives.

Gandhi believed that there is no religion higher than truth and righteousness and true religion along with morality are inseparable. He rejected any religious doctrine that did not appeal to reason and was in conflict with morality. Without moral basis, one ceases to be religions. It's true, however, that God can not be wicked, untruthful, cruel and incontinent. He is not supposed to have immoral selfish desires.

A truly religious person should ceaselessly work for the welfare of mankind.

Gandhi believed that religion is everybody's personal concern and the State has nothing to do with it. He swore by his religion and would die for it. He could not live for a single second without religion. For him, even the tiniest activity was governed by it. His political and other activities were inspired by religion. He thought politics without religion was dirt, even to be discarded. The religion, to him, meant being bound to God, that is to say, your every breath is regulated by God.

The concept of religion propounded by Gandhi takes into account, elements of ethics, morality, truth, non-violence, tolerance and similar other moral qualities to be practiced by a follower of religion. He considers non-violence as the supreme religious duty. In this way, love, kindness, feeling of universal brotherhood are the fundamentals of true religion which emphasizes the service of mankind. He wanted to harmonise all religions in order to establish the kingdom of God on earth.

Aesthetics of Gandhi

The general impression about Gandhi Ji was that he was puritanic and priestly type and he was without aesthetic inclination. But this view was not really correct. He was not a dry or dreadful person, without humour or any appreciation or idea of beauty and art. In his own words, he was a 'jolly good fellow'.

Gandhi considered Art as an essential aspect of human life. He showed admiration and reverence for beautiful things, flowers, plants etc. He did not like people plucking delicate flowers to shower on his face or to hang around his neck. He would love watching the beauty of nature, whenever free from his social and political pursuits. He was concerned with all time arts, music, poetry, painting, drama, sculpture, dance, literature etc. He was delighted to watch the play of Tagore and thrilled to hear good Bhajans. He felt music in life, in walking, in instruments and even in the marching of soldiers. While in England, he also developed taste for Western music and liked plays of Shakespeare. From England, he went on a visit to Paris to see the great exhibition in 1890. He was impressed by the beauty, grandeur and peacefulness of ancient churches in Paris. He admired the wonderful architecture of Notre Dame with its elaborate interior decoration and beautiful sculpture.

Poetry also fascinated Gandhi and sometimes he would write a letter in a poetic language. Dance and music were a source of sweetness in life for him. He was captirated by religions paintings and architecture and felt love of God in the heart of those who were responsible for those wonderful pieces of arts. He liked the beauty of Taj Mahal and Ajanta paintings. After attending the Round Table Conferance in London, he visited Rome and admired paintings and sculpture of its famous Cathedral.

His opinion of Art transcended the common concept of art. For him, even the search for Truth and the practice of Yoga was an art.

Asceticism, for him was the greatest of all arts. He found beauty in truth and through truth. According to him, there are two aspects of things, the outward and the inward. The outwards has no meaning if it does not help the inward. He, therefore, believed that all true art is thus the expression of the soul. The true value of outward forms, therefore, lies in the right expression of the inner self in man. He believed that all true art must help the soul to realize its inner self.

Gandhi did not support the popular prevalent theory 'ART for arts sake'. He strongly believed that art has a purpose which is moral and spiritual. It should spread harmony in an individual and the society. He felt that art and religion should go together. He opined that art should be an instrument to serve mankind. However, he did not refuse to accept the value of forms of art generally accepted as such, but he found them inadequate when compared with the eternal symbols of beauty in nature. No conscious art of man could produce the panoramic scenes of starry heavens overhead that display an unending expanse of natural beauty. The productions of man-made art are valuable only so far as they help the soul towards self-realization.

For Gandhi, good art was not the monopoly of a few but is good for all. For him singing of RAM DHUN in unison and harmony was an art. Once he said, "I want art and literature that can speak to the millions. Real work of art should appeal to all. It must be joy for all. It should work for the welfare of all." He declared that "Life is greater than art." He even went further to say that "the man whose life comes nearest to perfection is the greatest artist; for what is art without the sure foundation and framework of a NOBLE LIFE."

Manual Labour and Gandhi

Gandhi Ji believed that each day every one should do some manual labour. Only brain work was not enough. Gradually, he changed his way of life and started doing any work that came in his way. In his ashram, he led a simple community life with other inmates and all lived like hard working, self-reliant companions. No paid servants were employed.

He always lent a helping hand in all types of jobs whether in the ashram or on the farm, whether it was building a hut, or a road, cooking, sweeping, carpentry, leather work, stitching clothes etc. Early morning, he would grind wheat in a hand mill then dress up and walk five miles to reach his office in Africa. He would clip his own hair, wash or iron his clothes. He would not feel ashamed to clean latrines. He was good at finding books and would assist in working a hand-driven printing machine. He wrote articles for his Journal or the press, type himself and composed them in his own printing press. He spun on a charkha, wove on a loom, cooked in the kitchen tended vegetable plants and fruit trees, and helped in tilling of land and unloading of heavy load from a cart. While in jail, he would dig hard land with a pickaxe and sew torn clothes and blankets for nine hours a day. In South Africa, he would keep awake a whole night nursing the plague-stricken minors. He had no hesitation in washing the wounds of a leper.

Gandhi was very fond of walking. In South Africa, he would walk five miles a day to reach his office of barrister. As a voluntary stretcher-bearer, he carried wounded soldiers, 30 to 40 miles. Once he walked 55 miles in one day. More than once, he walked 40 miles a day to buy things from a store. Even at 78, he worked for 18 hours a day and sometimes for 21 hours. Even at that age, he would walk 3-5 miles a day, during winters.

Gandhi learnt scavenging in South Africa. His friends lovingly called him the great scavenger. In India, all scavenging work in his ashram was done by the inmates and Gandhi guided them. He introduced several innovations in sanitation work and on many occasions called himself as a bhangi. His advice was "If you become your own scavenger, you will make your surroundings clean." He would set an example by himself using bucket and broom with pride. He wanted to lift scavenging from its low level to the level of indispensable social work.

Gandhi Ji tried his hands at all sorts of manual work. He did scavenging, acted as barber, tailor, cobbler, washer man, nurse and even as mid-wife. In his ashram, he performed different kinds of work generally done by the menials. He felt no shame in doing any type of manual labour, including cleaning of kitchen utensils, cleaning vegetables and doing other odd jobs.

In short, he had tremendous energy and determination for doing any type of manual work and knew no fatigue. He was ready to do anything that was not beyond his capacity.

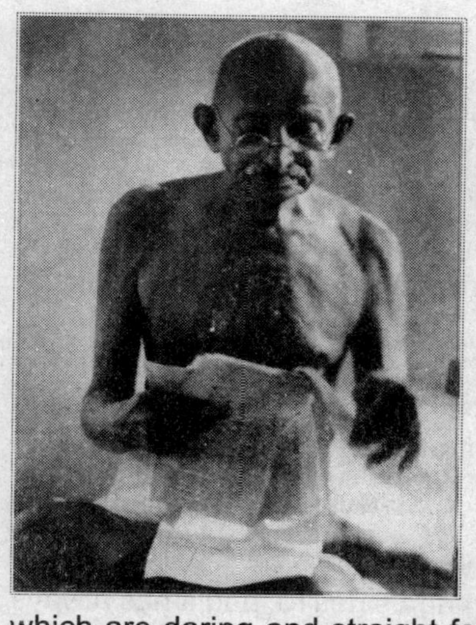

Miscellaneous Thoughts of Gandhi

In his autobiography and some other writings, Gandhi has made several critical and interesting comments which are daring and straight forward. No ordinary mortal would have done that. Most people below their own trumpet and try to exaggerate whatever small goodness they have in them. It goes to the credit of Gandhi that he admitted even his weakness and deficiencies which, of course, he overpowered as he grew in life. We give below some of the comments made by Gandhi on himself and other things in his own words.

On His Early Life

I used to be shy and avoided all company. My books and my lessons were my sole companion.

I had not any high regard for my ability. I used to be astonished whenever I won prizes and scholarship. But I very jealously guarded my character.

I was a coward. I used to he haunted by the fear of thieves, ghosts and serpents. I did not dare to stare out of doors at night. Darkness was terror to me.

Becoming Vegetarian

I may claim to have become a vegetarian by choice. I was blessed the day on which I had taken the vow (not to take meat) infront of my mother.

I had gone to England, a convinced meat-eater, and was intellectually converted to vegetarianism.

Barrister's Job

I found the barrister's profession a bad job-much show and little knowledge. I never resorted to untruth in my profession.

I realized what the true function of a lawyer was to unite parties driven asunder.

Service of the poor has been my heart's desire, and it has always thrown me amongst the poor and enabled me to identify with them.

I had made the religion of service my own as I felt that God could be realized only through service.

Humour

If I had no sense of humour, I should long ago have committed suicide.

Sanskrit

I am not a profound scholar of Sanskrit. I have read the VEDAS and the UPANISHADS only in translations.

Virtue

The only virtues I want to claim is truth and non-violence. I have no claim to super human powers. I want none.

On Being Mahatma

The mahatma I leave to his fate. I shall gladly subscribe to a bill to make it criminal for anybody to call me mahatma and to touch my feet. Truth to me is dearer them 'MAHATMASHIP', which is purely a burden.

His life

My life has been an open book. I have no secrets and encourage no secrets.

Prestige

I have no desire for prestige anywhere. It is furniture required in courts of kings.

Hate

I hold myself incapable of hating any being an earth. I know this is a big claim I make it in all humility.

Truth

Truth to me is infinitely dearer than the 'mahatmaship'.

Wealth Of Gandhi

I am a poor medicant. My earthly possessions consist of six spinning wheels, prison dishes, a can of goats milk, six home-spun lion clothes and towels and my reputation which can not be worth much!

I came to the conclusion that if I have to serve the people in whose midst my life was cast and of whose difficulties I was a witness from day to day. I must discard all wealth, all possessions.

My Sins

I have made the frankest admission of many sins. But I do not carry their burden on my shoulders.

On Gandhism

There is no such thing as 'Gandhism' and I do not want to leave any seet after me. I do not claim to have originated any new principle or doctrine. I have simply tried in my own way to apply the eternal truth to our daily life and problems.

On Himself

By instinct I have been truthful but not violent. I have no secrets of my own in this life. I have owned my weaknesses. If I were sexsually inclined, I would have the courage to make the confession. I am not a STATESMAN in the garb of a saint.

I am but a seeker after Truth. I am an humble but very earnest seeker of Truth.

I may be a despicable person, but when Truth speaks through me, I am invincible. I have in my life never been guilty of saying things I did not mean.

I claim to be no more than an average man with less than average ability.

I lay claim to nothing exclusively divine in me. I do not claim prophet-ship.

I am an irrepressible optimist.

I am not a visionary, I claim to be a practical idealist.

I admit my limitations. I have no university education worth the name. My high school career was never above the average. I was thankful if I could pass my examinations.

I look upon myself as a dull person. I take more time than others in understanding some things.

I have been an obedient son to my parents and an equally obedient pupil to my teachers.

I believe in the absolute oneness of God and therefore of humanity.

I know of no greater sin then to oppress the innocent in the name of God.

Image Of Gandhi

I read a newspaper cutting sent by a correspondent to the effect that a temple has been created where my image is being worshipped. This I consider to be a gross form of idolatry.

On His Death

I do not want to die of a creeping paralysis of my faculties-a defeated man. An assasin's bullet may put an end to my life. I would welcome it. But I would love, above all, to fade out doing my duty with my last breath.

If I die of a lingering illness, may even as a boil or a pimple, it will be your duty to proclaim to the world, even at the risk of making people angry, that I was not the man of God that I claimed to be.

On Rebirth

I do not want to be reborn. But if I have to be reborn, I should be born an untouchable, so that I may share their sorrows, sufferings and affronts leveled at them.

The Highest Honour

The highest honour that my friends can do me is to enforce in their own lives the programme that I stand for or to resist me to their utmost if they not believe in it.

Views On Miscellaneous Matters

My life consists of nothing but my numerous experiment, with TRUTH.

The title of MAHATMA has little value for me and often it has deeply pained me.

What I want to achieve is self-realization.

The essence of Religion is morality.

My life is one indivisible whole, and all my activities run into one another.

I have insatiable love of mankind.

True friendship is an identity of souls rarely to be found in this world.

The wife is not the husband's bond slave.

Truth is the substance of all morality.

I regard untouchability as the greatest blot on Hinduism.

I may claim to have become vegetarian by choice.

Service of the poor has been my heart's desire.

The education of the child begins with conception.

The act of generation should be controlled for the ordered growth of the world.

Control of the palate is the first essential in the observance of brahmacharya.

Truth is like a vast tree which yields more and more fruit the more you nurture it.

Ahimsa is the basis of the search for truth.

The sole aim of Journalism should be service.

One should not eat in order to please the palate but just to keep the body going.

Fasting can help to curb animal passion, only if it is undertaken with a view to self-restraint.

I had heard that a lawyer's profession is a liar's profession. I never resorted to untruth in my progession.

For me non-violence is not a mere philosophical principle. It is the rule and the breath of my life.

The only virtues I want to claim are truth and non-violence. I lay no claim to suffer human powers.

My life has been an open book. I have no secrets and I encourage no secrets.

The only means to the realization of truth is Ahimsa.

Ahimsa is the farthest limit of humility.

I have no desire for prestige anywhere.

I hold myself incapable of hating any being on earth.

Jesus to me is a great world teacher among others.

There is no dharma higher than truth.

Non-violence is the highest duty.

All our relationships are the result of the sanskaras we carry from our previous births.

As the means so the end.

Ahimsa is the means, Truth is the end.

Socialism is a beautiful word and so far as I am aware, in socialism all the members of society are equal - none low, none high.

Love is the strongest force the world possesses and yet it is the highest imaginable.

Life is an aspiration. Its mission is to strive after perfection which is self-realization.

True happiness is impossible without true health and true health is impossible without a rigid control of the palate.

Moral result can only he produced by moral restraints.

Experience teaches that animal food is unsuited to those who would curb their passions.

Experience has taught me that silence is a part of the spiritual discipline.

He is silent who, having the capacity to speak, utters no idle word.

Sex urge is a fine and noble thing. But it is meant only for the act of creation.

Mind is at the root of all sensuality.

All men are equal in God's eyes.

The world is my family.

My goal is friendship with the whole world.

I would not like to live in the world if it is not to be one world.

A starving man thinks first on satisfying his hunger before anything else.

I would say that if the village perishes, India will perish too. India will be no more India.

God created man to work for his food and said that those who ate without work were thieves.

For the poor the economics is the spiritual.

Every man has an equal right to the necessities of life even as birds and beasts have. But every right carries with it a corresponding duty.

My nation of democracy is that under which the weakest should have the same opportunity as the strongest.

The time source of rights is duty.

Democracy disciplined and enlightened is the finest thing in the world.

Democracy and violence can not go together.

Every good movement passed through five stages, indifference ridicule, abuse, repression and respect.

Real education consists in drawing the best out of yourself.

By education I mean an all round drawing out of the best in child and man - body, mind and spirit.

My House

I do not want my house to be walled in on all sides and my windows to be stuffed. I want the cultures of all lands to be blown about my house as freely as possible. But I refuse to blow off my feet by any.

Music means rhythms, order. Its effect is electrical. It immediately soothes.

The eyes, the ears, the tongue come before the hand. Reading comes before writing and drawing before tracing.

India's salvation depends on the sacrifice and enlightenment of her women.

Ahimsa means infinite love, which again means infinite capacity for suffering.

Women is the personification of self-sacrifice.

To call woman the weaker sex is a libel, it is pure and religions in life.

Marriage is natural thing in life. In Hinduism, it is one of the four ASHRAMS of life, on which the other three are based.

My humble occupation has been to show people how they can solve their own difficulties.

It is better in prayer to have a heart without words than words without a heart.

The weak can never forgive. Forgiveness is the attribute of the strong.

The greatest men of world have always stood alone - Take the great prophets, Buddha, Jesus, Muhammad - they all stood alone like many other.

No matter how insignificant the thing you have to do, do it as well as you can, give it as much of your care and attention as you would give to the thing you regard as most important.

Goodness must be joined with knowledge. Mere goodness is not of much use.

Everything created by God animate or inanimate has its good side and bad side.

True ahimsa should mean a complete freedom from ill-will anger and hate and an overflowing love for all.

Constant development is the law of life.

Man is the maker of his destiny in the sense that he has the freedom of choice as to the manner in which he uses his freedom. But he is no controller of results.

It is a bad habit to say that another mans thoughts are bad and ours only are good and that those holding different views from ours are the enemies of the country.

I do not want to foresee the future. I am concerned with taking care of present. God has given me no control over the moment following.

Love And Hatred

Hatred ever kills, love never dies, such is the vast difference between the two.

What is obtained by love is retained for all times.

What is obtained by hatred proves a burden in reality for it increases hatred.

Traits Most Dangerous To Humanity

Wealth without work.

Pleasure without conscience.

Science without humanity.

Knowledge without character.

Politics without principles.

Commerce without morality.

Worship without sacrifice.

According to Gandhi Ji, non-violence is the greatest force at the disposal of mankind. It is mightier than the mightiest weapon of destruction devised by the ingenuity of man.

Part – 3

- Gandhi and Kasturba

Gandhi and Kasturba

It is quite interesting to note that Gandhi and his wife Kasturba were born in the same town of Porbandar (in Gujarat State) in the same year 1869. She was a few months older than Gandhi Ji.

Her maiden name was Kastur Kapadia. After her marriage, she become Kasturba Gandhi. In later life, she became Kasturba or mere Ba, which means 'Great Mother' and Gandhi became 'Bapu'. She had two brothers, one elder and one younger, and was the middle child of a wealthy parents. The house of Gandhi and Kapadia families were located in the same lane and it is presumed that both Gandhi and Kasturba might have played together as children. She did not go to school, but she learnt the art of being a married woman and housekeeper, in the home of her parents. She also learnt the stories of ancient Indian's mythical pious ladies like Savitri, Anusuya, Sita and Taramati, all of whom were Indian idols and faithful model wives.

In the year 1876, when both Gandhi and Kasturba were seven years old, their betrothal was arranged when both were quite ignorant of the significance of that event. At the ceremony, while she received some nice presents, Gandhi was not even physically present and he was told about it later. Their actual marriage took place in 1882, six years after the betrothal ceremony. Both were about the same age of thirteen years when they were married. Together they took seven steps and vows of marriage rites, without knowing the special meaning of the words uttered by them, as instructed by the priest.

On their first night, Gandhi Ji later described as follows:

"And oh! that first night. Two innocent children, all unwillingly hurled themselves into the ocean of life". He further mentioned "We were too nervous to face each other. And we were certainly too shy. How was I to talk to her and what was I to say?"

At the time of their marriage, both of them knew very little about sex. But they gradually began to know each other and to speak freely. In his own words, much later, Gandhi said "I do not think, it (marriage) meant to me anything more than the prospect of good clothes to wear, drum beating, marriage processions, rich dinners and a strange girl to play with. The carnal desire come later."

Gandhi and Kasturba embarked on the adventure of marriage as shy, strange playmates without understanding the significance of their relationship and in total ignorance of its sexual aspect. However, slowly they began to know each other and to speak freely with each other.

While Mohandas returned to High school, they could only be together late at night as Kasturba also remained busy in household chores, during the day. Gandhi was passionately fond of Kasturba and even at school, he used to think of her. Separation from her was unbearable and the thought of nightfall and their meeting always hunted him. Although they were of the same age, Gandhi soon assumed the authority of a husband and started playing the role of a typical dominant Indian husband possessive and at the same time, jealous of his wife. With this background, one day he told Kasturba not to go out of the house without his permission. Proud and free as she was, she found this dictate as embarrassing and humiliating. While she did not openly object to this, she made no promise to observe his instruction. The very next day she went to the temple, with his mother-in-law without the permission of Gandhi. She repeated similar outside visits, without permission even on subsequent days and this provoked Mohandas who tried to impose more restrictions. But Kasturba reacted strongly and said "Should I obey you or your mother?"

And Gandhi became helpless after hearing this.

She argued further, "If some elders ask me to go out with them, should I tell them, that I can't do this without my husband's permission."

Consequently, Gandhi realized that he could not impose his undue authority on Kasturba and therefore, resumed normal behaviour.

As Kasturba was illiterate, like any other Indian woman during these days, her zealous husband chalked out a plan to teach her. The only time available for this was at night. But each night, they would abandon the efforts and go to bed as Gandhi was overpowered by his passion to make love to his wife. Kasturba too after having been tried of days routine, had neither the energy nor the aptitude to study. So the experiment of teaching his wife failed. During later years, Gandhi attributed the failure to his weakness of 'Lustful love'.

During his school days, Mohandas come into close contact with a Muslim school mate, named Mehtab Sheikh. Gandhi was greatly impressed by him as he was very strong, well built and excelled in sports. As Mohan started spending too much time with him, Kasturba was greatly distressed by their friendship and warned her husband against this but he disregarded her advice and continued his relationship.

However, later on, Gandhi regarded this friendship as a tragedy in his life, because of its several evil consequences. This showed that Kasturba was perceptive judge of human character. She gave her husband solace and sympathy which he needed most when he indulged in his indiscretions but confessed all to Kasturba.

Whole family became happy when they learnt that Kasturba was expecting her first child. The child was born prematurely and died after a few days of birth. Mohan blamed this due to his reckless self-indulgence and years later, he wrote in his autobiography

‘Nothing else could be expected’. Kasturba felt guilty but she never discussed the matter with anyone, but she carried the thrust of hidden sorrow for the loss of her first-born. However, in due course, she recovered her self-confidence which helped her heal her wound.

During 1888, it was decided to send Mohandas to UK for studies in law. On September 4, 1888, he left Bombay and sailed for England, while Kasturba was left in Rajkot to feel lonely for three years. However, before the departure of Mohan, their second son was born who kept her busy and made her life sweet. She also found great comfort in her relationship with her mother-in-law. In view of difficult family financial circumstances, she cut down expenditure on her comforts which included even food and clothes. However, she would make sweets to send to Mohan in London. For Kasturba, England was a mysterious place and she wondered how her husband was living there. Since she could not read, she was deprived of the benefit of knowing anything through his letter which were addressed to his brother and news about Mohan trickled down to her only through her sister-in-law. Thus, this separation from her husband with whose she could not ever communicate through a letter was, perhaps, the hardest for her to bear. She often thought and waited for the day when she would meet her husband again.

While Mohan was still in England, the Gandhi family faced a tragedy of unexpected death of Putlibai, Mohan’s dear mother. However, the sad news was not conveyed to him. With her death, Kasturba was sad of great grief and uncertainty and was deprived of her mother-in-law’s love, guidance and loving protection. She exercised great patience and waited anxiously to have the first glimpse of her husband.

When Gandhi returned from England, Kasturba found him changed in many ways but she was delighted to know that he had not forgotten her. But his insistence upon Kasturba to take lessons again was not to her liking and the effort did not prove successful. As the family was down with financial difficulties, she would remind her husband about the dues he owed to his brothers. This angered Mohan who then sent her and his son to her parents home. However, he called her back within a month. She was also not pestered with the teaching of lessons any more, but she became, more concerned about her husband's anxieties. When he confided his fears to her she not only listened attentively but also consoled him and encouraged him for appropriate action. When Mohan went to Bombay to seek better avenues, she stood by him and expressed her good wishes.

Meanwhile, another son was born to Kasturba and this was a cause for rejoicing. However, Mohan did not fare better at Bombay and he was called back home, where he opened a new office and started earning some income. This was cause of success for Kasturba and she was content and happier, as never before.

In 1893, Gandhi was offered a lucrative job in South Africa, which meant another separation from Kasturba, though only for one year. Being optimist and hopeful of her husband's success, she fully supported him in this new venture. In south Africa, Gandhi encountered difficulties, learnt many lessons but fulfilled his job successfully. Some local developments later demanded his presence in South Africa, so he extended his stay there longer. This came as a mixture of hope and fear to Kasturba who became more troubled by the further absence of his husband. She suffered from some uncertainty and apprehensions, as by then though they had been married for about eleven years, they had stayed together only for about four year. While she herself could tolerate this separation, she was more concerned from the side of her sons who were growing and were deprived of their father's affection. While these concerns hunted her, she always prayed for her husband's safe return from a distant hand overseas. Such was her concern for her husband, his success and welfare in spite of her own suffering and sacrifice.

While Gandhi stayed in South Africa for a couple of years more he was always occupied in her thoughts and she was always worried about him. The activities of Gandhi increased many fold, his law practice flourished and he become well off-financially. After around three years, he decided to return to India for a six months vacation.

When he returned to Rajkot, he become extremely busy because of his involvement in South Africa and Kasturba always longed to have more time with him but she did not have the heart to tell him so. The South African experience had brought tremendous change in Mohandas while Kasturba was the same unchanging self. She wondered about the life in South Africa.

When Mohandas returned to South Africa with his family he met a hostile crowd because of certain wrong propaganda against him. This dismayed Kasturba who feared greatly for her husband and the family. After facing several hazards, Gandhi and his family ultimately got settled in their own home in Durban. Kasturba was overjoyed to be in her own new home, which was a beautiful European style villa never seen by her before. However, she found herself in an entirely new surroundings and missed the lively and familiar environment of Rajkot.

A strange and unusual incident happened while living in the house. Several of Gandhi's young low clerks were also living in the some house. Each morning all residents were required to empty chamber pots from their own rooms. In case any pots were neglected, Gandhi would clean these pots and would also require Kasturba to join him in this work. This requirement filled her with anger and disgust, besides shame. The situation became terrible when a new arrival, an untouchable Christian of Indian origin, unaware of the custom in the house, left his chamber pot under his bed. Weeping and full of anger she carried the pot away to empty it. Mohan who was watching her knowing that she was not doing this job gladly, shouted at her, "I will not stand this nonsense in my home."

His words hurt her and she recoiled, "keep your home to yourself and let me go." This annoyed Gandhi who caught her and dragged her to the gate and wanted to push her out. At this, she burst out and cried, "Have you no sense of shame? Where am I to go I have no parents or relations who will take care of me here." Mohan felt ashamed and shut the gate. He knew that if his wife could not leave him, he should neither leave her. In spite of numerous such quarrels they had, the end was always peaceful and Kasturba by dint of her tolerance and silent sufferings was always the winner. Later in his autobiography, Gandhi described this incident in a very touching and painful manner and called himself a 'cruelly kind husband'. He claimed himself as his wife's teacher and the harassment which he caused to her was out of great love for her. Later he also felt sorry for disregarding the feelings of his wife. This ugly incident, however, taught a great lesson to both of them and they together vowed never to repeat it again.

Sometime later, when another baby was born to Kasturba, Gandhi in the absence of proper medical facilities himself acted as a nurse and an attendant to look after his bed ridden wife, the new born and other sons. Such was his concern for her wife that he helped her in any manner required during the labour and after the birth when she was convalescing. He also looked after Kasturba very well, on the occasion of the birth of their fourth son, when no medical help was available and he acted as mid-wife.

A time came when she realized her husbands desire for sexual abstinence. On his suggestion, they started sleeping in separate leads and Kasturba had no objection and agreed without making any comment. On return to India, Gandhi met the leaders of National congress and thereafter decided to travel throughout India in third class by train to acquaint himself with conditions prevailing in the country. The trip back to India was both of pleasure and grief for Kasturba. She was happy to be among the welcoming relatives at Rajkot but sad to experience the absence of her parents and others at Porbandar. After some hard thinking, Gandhi decided to settle in Bombay. For Kasturba, this meant to adjust once again to a new life but she felt at home being in her own country, India. But this state did not last long as Gandhi was again called back in South Africa in view of urgent and demanding circumstances. This time he went alone leaving Kasturba and the family back in India. This meant again a life of doubts and uncertainty but she stood by her husband to meet the cell of duty. Sometime later, Gandhi called Kasturba and children (except Hari Lal who wanted to continue his studies in India) to join him in South Africa. Thus she had to adjust with the changes of life, again. In their new life and circumstances at a new places where the professional and social engagements of Gandhi increased day by day, Kasturba played the significant role of a perfect helpmate to him. It was then that he was quite surprised to know about her hidden strength providing unexpected support and also realized her compassion and capacity to help the distressed people of her own relation. The crisis brought out the true nature of Kasturba to the fore. In South Africa, Kasturba whcleheartedly supported Gandhi in all his new ventures in the public service and she enjoyed working with other people who were also engaged in their tasks.

In was in South Africa, that he took the vow of Brahmacharya in consultation with Kasturba who had no objection. With this vow they started a new phase of their life and Gandhi felt more free to attend to the calls of public service. By now she knew that her husband was an extraordinary person and she was ready to follow him and was sustained by the faith of a Hindu wife.

Gandhi's son Hari Lal, who was left behind in India for studies got married to Gulab without the knowledge of his parents. Gandhi wanted their marriage at tater stage so he was unhappy. However at Kasturba's persuasions he reconciled to the happening and extended his blessings to the young couple. On Kasturba's urging they come to visit their parents. While an important festive event was being organized in their home, news come that Gandhi was arrested by the local white rulers as he was espousing the righteous came of the local Indians in defiance of the unjust local regulations. This happened when everyone was enjoying a festive meal and Kasturba was about to start eating. On hearing the grim news she shopped the celebration and did not eat the special dishes. She pushed her plate away. She felt that while she could not share her husband's hardships in jail, she could at least share his diet. Until Gandhi was released, she ate only unsalted, tasteless food like of which was served to him in jail. This strict pledge she took herself to express her solidarity with her husband in his distress. While Gandhi was in prison, she was worried and had fears about his safety. It was her full faith in God that reassured her and she was overjoyed when Gandhi was freed from prison.

While in South Africa, Kasturba whose health was deteriorating, once fell seriously ill and the doctor advised that she should take beef broth otherwise she will not survive. This was against the Hindu religions practice and both Gandhi and Kasturba were against it. The doctor persisted but Kasturba resisted and did not agree to doctor's advice of taking meat. Later, she became better. Such was the great courage of Kasturba and Gandhi fully supported her.

Gandhi was concerned about Kasturba's health as she was weak and frail. He had read somewhere that frail people should avoid all forms of beans, lentils and other legumes. He wanted to try diet free of these elements on Kasturba who disagreed with this view and thought that food helped build the body. She asked Gandhi to try this experiment on herself and said, "Why don't you give up lentils yourself before advising others." This she said light heartedly but Gandhi took it very seriously and vowed, "Ok, I will give up all such dishes for one year starting from today."

Kasturba did not mean this, so she was taken aback and told him, "No, you don't do this. I was joking." But Gandhi was unable to take back his vow. So they both started with their new diet plan together. Fortunately, the condition of Kasturba improved.

Unfortunately the relations between Gandhi and his son, Hari Lal became strained. Hari Lal had to go to Jail because of his father's movement and also had some other personal grievances. Kasturba tried to resolve their conflict but could not do much. Hari Lal, therefore, returned to India as he thought that his father did not care for them. His going back to India caused much anxiety to Kasturba. Sometime later, she also had to go to Jail for the cause for which her husband had been struggling and suffering. She did that willingly and without any pressure from Gandhi.

Gandhi's pursuit of ideals sometimes hurt others whom he wanted to teach or reform and in his zeal he was being stubborn or even unfair. Kasturba used her own method of silent persuasion to bring about change in his stern attitude.

Gandhi ji and Kasturba

Her quiet behaviour was in the true spirit of Satyagraha which impressed Gandhi who once remarked, "I learned the lesson of non-violence from my wife." She brought change is him by suffering herself. In this way she exerted an effective on her husband in her own way.

When Gandhi became seriously ill and suffered from severe pain also, doctor advised surgery for which he was required to gain body strength. He was advised to take milk which long time earlier he had vowed not to take in view of the cruelty to animals, involved in the process of getting milk by greedy farmer. However Kasturba came with a ready solution when she suggested that he could take goats milk, arguing that when Gandhi took the vow, he must had in his mind, milk of cow or buffalo, which is of course a fact. So this is how Gandhi agreed to take goats milk. In this way, he could keep his vow as well as, drink goats milk. The operation was thus performed and Gandhi became well under the care and attention given by his wife.

In response to Gandhi's non-cooperation movement against the British rules, the latter sentenced him to six years imprisonment. She was with him at the great trial and accompanied him to Sabarmati Jail. Next day she veined an appeal to the men and women of India to carry on the constructive program of the congress based on Gandhi's convictions.

While Gandhi was undergoing sentence in prison, Kasturba took charge of the activities in Sabarmati Ashram. While Gandhi in prison pondered over the destiny of the people of India, his wife worried about him and also the family going through personal travail and turmoils.

During greater part of her life, kasturba followed her husband like a shadow. She helped him in every possible way and played the role of a most devoted wife. She shared his anxieties, attended to him in illness. Suffered with him in all problems of their life and was often jailed with him. However, she was also equally strong-minded as her husband and she had the courage to resist his unjust demands, sometime. A time also came when she was charting her own course more and more, dispelling any notion that she blindly followed her husband's every dictate. She had an independent nature from the start of their married life but, oven the years when she came much closer to her husband and understood him more fully. She merged her personality with his and sacrificed her wishes and needs for his cause and activities. With the passage of time, she learned to read a little but always resisted Gandhi's attempts to give her formal tuition. While Gandhi was extremely strict about rules and his principles of life, Kasturba was more lenient and loving in dealing with their associates.

As a result of strenuous life, Kasturba had to lead in view of Gandhi's involvement in public service and later in the movement for the freedom of India. Kasturba had to go through great suffering. Her health, therefore, in later life became a matter of concern on frequent occasions. As she was aging, she was ailing and at times, became very ill. Inspite of that she was filled with devotion and kindness.

While she was imprisoned with Gandhi in Aga khan place, she felt seriously ill and felt that her time was up. Gandhi was with her when the end came close. She looked peaceful and smiling meekly at Bapu said, "There should be no weeping and mourning. My death should be an occasion for rejoicing." She then closed her eyes and said some prayer. A few hours later, she stopped breathing. She was no more. While standing near her burning pyre, Gandhi said, "The best half of me is dead. What am I going to do now?" At one point he expressed, "I cannot ever imagine life without Ba. She was an indivisible part of me, and her going has left a void which will never be filled."

Part - 4

- Some more Memorable Incidents from the Life of Gandhi

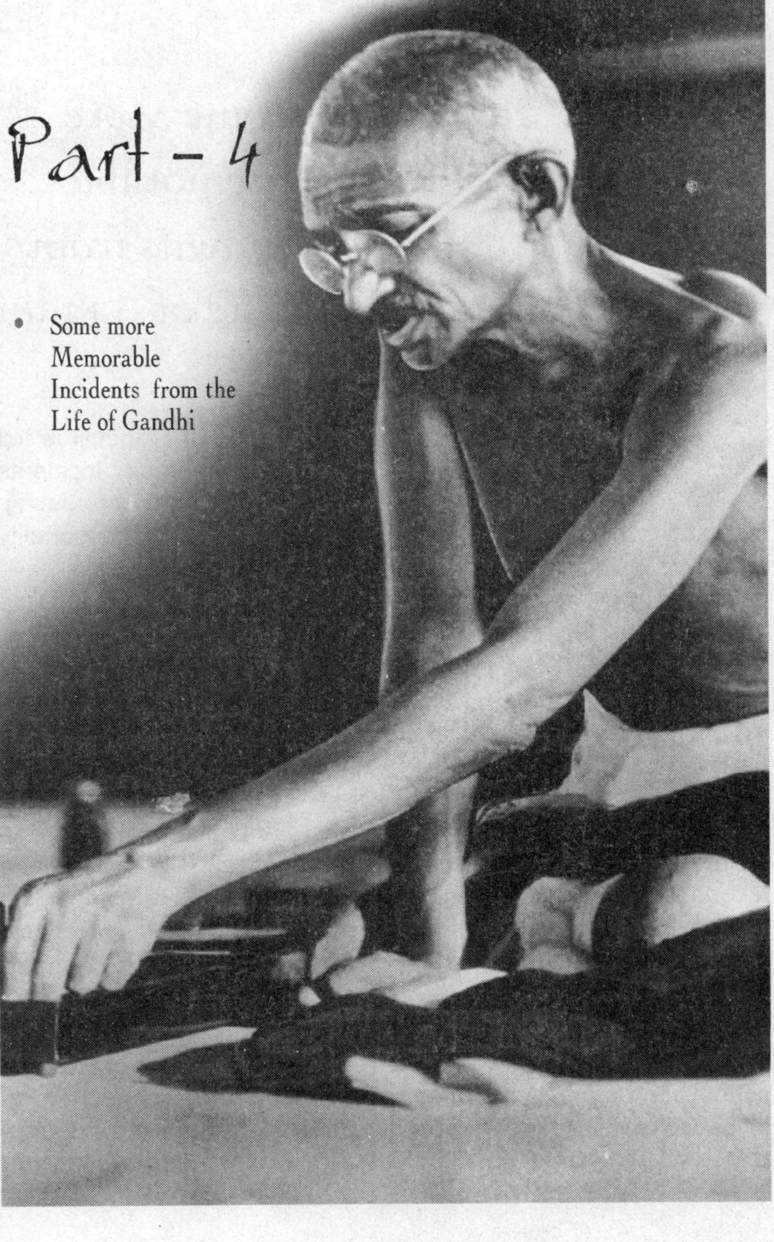

Some More Memorable Incidents from the Life of Gandhi

The life of Gandhiji is full of numerous incidents which are interesting, instructive, inspiring and memorable. These reveal his personality and have also contributed to the shaping of his later life. We have collected these incidents from various sources, as far a possible and the same are briefly described below:-

Truthfulness

Truthfulness was the special characteristic of Gandhi even in his childhood. Once his playmates decided to steal idols of god and goddesses from a temple to play a game. The priest woke up while the children were busy doing their job. He chased them but the children hid the idols somewhere and ran away. The priest made a complaint to Gandhi's uncle who interrogated the boys including Gandhiji. While the other boys lied and professed ignorance, Gandhi spoke the truth and told all that he knew.

School Incident – Against Cheating

This incident occurred while Gandhi was in first year of the high school. The education inspector had come to the school on an inspections visit. He gave five words to write as a spelling exercise; one word was 'KETTLE'. Gandhi spelt it wrong. When his teacher noticed this, he tried to prompt Gandhi to copy the correct spelling from another student. Gandhi did not do this as he thought that this would be cheating. The result was that all the boys except Gandhi spelt the word correctly. The teacher reprimanded Gandhi who never learnt copying.

Uka—the Untouchable

Gandhi was hardly twelve, when he came face to face with an incident of untouchability. A scavenger, named Uka used to come to the house for cleaning latrines. He was considered untouchable and Gandhi was instructed not to touch him. He would often ask his mother why it was wrong to touch Uka. Incase Gandhi accidentally touched him, he was made to take bath, under protest, as he considered that untouchability was not sanctioned by religion. As a dutiful and obedient child Gandhi would obey his parents but he often had tussle with them on this matter. He would tell his mother that she was entirely wrong in considering physical contact with Uka as sinful.

Later in life, Gandhi became the greatest champion of the untouchable and called them 'Harijans' - men of God. He regarded untouchability as the greatest blot on Hinduism.

How Gandhi Was Ex-communicated

On the advice of an old family friend, it was decided to send Gandhi to UK to study law. Going across the ocean was considered against religion during those days. Therefore, the caste elders asked Gandhi to appear before the Vania (community) council. Gandhi did so and argued that he had already taken a vow not to eat meat etc., but they did not agree. Gandhi was bold enough and refused to submit to the irrational and orthodox exercise of authority of the community elders and therefore, did not cancel his visit to UK. He was, therefore, declared outcaste. This is how, he was ex-communicated.

Another Insulting Incident

While in Pretoria, Gandhi used to walk through President Street to an open space. President's house was located in this street and a police patrol was always there. He would always go past the patrol along the foot path without any hindrance.

One day a man on duty, without any warning or without asking him to leave, pushed and kicked him into the street. Gandhi was dismayed. Mr. Coates who lived there and knew Gandhi, happened to be passing that way on house back and he noticed this incident. He advised Gandhi to proceed against the errant policeman and himself offered to be a witness. But Gandhi declined and said, "I have made it a rule not to go to court in respect of any personal grievance. I do not intend to proceed against him."

This incident deepened Gandhi's feelings for Indians in South Africa and he become more determined to bring about improvement in their living social conditions.

Gandhi's First Public Speech

The experiences of Gandhi in Pretoria gave him a fairly good idea of the social conditions of Indians in Transvaal and he wished to work for their welfare. With the help of some local acquaintances, he called a meeting of all Indians in the Transvaal capital and made a speech which may be said to have been his first public speech which was memorable. It was without any bitterness in spite of insulting and humiliating treatment faced by him from the white people. He dwelt on duties and obligations of Indian residents and exhorted them to observe truthfulness in business, cleanliness in personal habits and inculcate the spirit of cooperation and unity among themselves irrespective of religion, caste or community. He suggested the formation of an association of Indians to discuss their common problems and to defend their rights. Consequently, the association was formed and it worked for the welfare of the Indian residents there.

Gandhi's public life may be said to have commenced from this public meeting and he was then well on the way to perform greater public service without any emoluments.

Help To Tamil Man

Gandhi had hardly put in around three or four months legal practice in Natal when a Tamil man in tattered clothes and injured came to him weeping. He had been badly beaten by his employer. His name was Balasundaram, and he was serving as indenture under a reputed European settler in Durban.

Gandhi sent him to a doctor and got a certificate from him about the nature of injury. Then he took the injured man to the magistrate and submitted an affidavit. The magistrate issued summons against the employer. After this incident, the Indian labourers regarded Gandhi as their friend and well-wisher and they began to visit his office. In this way, Gandhi got an opportunity of learning their joys and sorrows. He thus found himself absorbed entirely in the service of the community and made service as his religion.

Respect For Mother's Conviction

Gandhi used to wear a necklace of Tulsi beads around his neck. This necklace was given to him by his mother out of her conviction that it would be conducive for his welfare. An acquaintance of Gandhi noticed it and thought it superstitious and wanted to break it. Gandhi did not permit as it was a sacred gift from his mother. He asked Gandhi, "but do you believe in it?"

Gandhi said, "I am not aware of its significance and I do not think harm will come to me if I do not wear it. But I can not discard it as my mother put it around my neck in the conviction that it would be conducive to my well being. However, when it breaks away on its own, I shall have no desire to replace it. But this necklace can not be broken."

And he did not replace it when the necklace wore out, in due course.

Physical Punishment To His Son

Gandhi was always opposed to corporal punishment. He remembered one occasion on which he physically punished one of his sons. He used the ruler but later was unable to judge whether he was right or wrong in doing that. However, he felt that it was improper as it was prompted by anger and a desire to punish.

Another Incident Of Punishment

In Tolstoy Farm in South Africa, Gandhi would teach boys there to speak the truth. One of the boy was unruly, quarrelsome and given to lying. One day he broke out most violently and this angered Gandhi who tried to reason with the boy but he was adamant. Gandhi hit the boy but trembled while he struck the boy. The boy cried and begged forgiveness as he realized the anguish of Gandhi Ji and thereafter he behaved well. But Gandhi Ji repented for his violent act.

Agony Of A Calf

A maimed calf lay in agony in the ashram of Gandhi Ji in spite of all nursing and possible treatment. The surgeon declared the case beyond help and hope. The animal was suffering from excruciating pain and could not even turn its side. In these circumstances, Gandhi Ji felt that the agony should end by ending its life.

Finally, in all humility but with clear conviction a killer injection was administered to end its agony as well as life. Gandhi Ji followed the right course which might appear wrong to some others.

Wealth Of Gandhi

Gandhi Ji once declared "I am a poor mendicant. My earthly possessions consist of six spinning wheels, prison dishes, a can of goat milk, six homespun loin-clothes and towels and my reputation which can not be worth much!"

First Experience Of Jail Life

Gandhi's first experience of jail life was in 1908, in South Africa which taught him to observe self-restraint. According to jail regulations, the last meal was to be finished before sunset and Indian and African prisons were not allowed tea or coffee. Nothing was served in the jail merely for the satisfaction of taste. Gandhi Ji found these rules useful for self-restraint. Even after release from jail Gandhi imposed these rules on himself. He stopped taking tea as far as it was then possible and finished his last meal before sunset. Later in life, these rules became his usual routine and no effort was required in their observance. It was a regular exercise in self-restraint.

In Yervada Jail

An incident in Yervada jail shows the humane aspect of Gandhi's personality. An African warder with life sentence was bitten by a scorpion and he was in great pain. Gandhi came to know about it and asked for a knife so that he could render some help. As the knife was not available he sucked the injured mans poison with his mouth and relieved the victim of the poison and his intense pain. This was an act of unselfish service for a sufferer.

Gandhian Humour

Humour was natural to Gandhi Ji. His smile was delightful, his laughter infectious and he reflected light heartedness. Once he told an interviewer that but for humour, he would have perhaps committed suicide! If his coworkers teased him for his strange habits, he would laugh that away. His experiments with neem leaves invited ridicule from a companion who said, "Bapu started with drinking goat's milk and now he has taken to goat's food!" Once while travelling in a car on an uneven road climbing and descending little mounds and ditches, he remarked that going on this road would improve any body's digestion. He would often exercise his sense of humour on himself. Once an artist showed him his portrait. Gandhi Ji looked at it and said, "Who is this monstrosity?" The artist replied yourself sir!

Return Of Medal

In appreciation of his social services, the government awarded KAISER-I-HIND medal to Gandhi Ji in 1915. But he did not feel comfortable on receiving a medal from an alien government as it put him in the rank of loyalists as against those who were undergoing hardships fighting for the freedom of the country. He also felt perturbed on hearing some sarcastic remarks on this subject from close companions. Gandhi Ji was therefore anxious to throw away this award. He found an opportune moment when he was ordered by the District Magistrate of Champaran to leave the district where he was doing public service. He returned the award to the Viceroy, saying "since government does not trust me enough to let me do public service in Champaran, it is not proper for me to keep the medal."

Love Of National Language

While speaking at the foundation ceremony of the Banaras Hindu University, Gandhi Ji felt sorry that he had to speak in English, since this was not the language understood by the masses. He expressed the view that English could not become the national language of India and it was necessary to develop our own national language for the development of our country.

Concern For All

Gandhi had great concern for the individual, for him no individual was small or insignificant. He gave advice to numerous individuals who sought it even for their personal problems.

Gandhi Ji said, "For me the smallest work is as important as the biggest."

Another Example

In retaliation to the riots in Bengal, there were communal riots in Bihar and Gandhi Ji went there to restore peace. It was then that the new Viceroy immediately on his arrival invited Gandhi Ji to Delhi offering his own plane to bring him. Gandhi Ji accepted the invitation but chose to travel by train. He felt disturbed that two train compartments were booked for him for his travel, one for preparing food and the other for his use and other activities. He immediately called the station master and surrendered one compartment for the use of poor passangers who were hanging to the windows.

A similar incident happened in Bengal, in 1945. Two compartments were booked for him and his team. Gandhi Ji thought that they all could be accommodated in one compartment, so he gave instructions to surrender other compartment. When he was told that the payment has already been made for two compartments, he said, "it does not matter. It does not allow us to enjoy comforts on the train when we are going for the service of the poor and the starving millions."

Gandhiji And Non-violence

Gandhiji used to take hot water mixed with lemon juice and some honey, early morning. His secretary Mahadev Desai would prepare this concoction for him. One day, while preparing this, the water was boiling too hot, so Mahadev kept it for cooling. As the water was boiling hot, steam started coming out of it. Gandhiji noticed this and said, "it would have been better, had you covered the pot." Mahadev said, "I thought it would cool down in five minutes and I am also observing that nothing falls into it."

Gandhiji said, "it is not the question of something falling into it. The hot steam coming out of it would needlessly harm some living entities in the air." Such was the concern of Gandhi Ji towards the safety and well being of other living creatures.

Gandhiji Met Tagore

Once Gandhi was guest of Rabindranath Tagore. Even though old, Tagore was a stickler for good looks and beauty. They were ready to go for evening walk, when Tagore said, "Please wait for a while, let me dress my hair." This surprised Gandhi who thought hair dressing at that old age quite senseless.

Tagore went inside and took considerable time for hair dressing. Gandhi peeped inside, saw Tagore standing in front of a full size mirror.

Gandhi said, "I don't understand why are you hair dressing at this old age. We are losing time for evening walk."

Tagore said, “When I was young, I would go without hair dressing, but in this old age, It has become necessary. Not that I wish to look handsome but I do not wish to become the cause of annoyance to anyone by looking shabby.”

Stay At Shanti Niketan

Gandhi and Tagore were contemporaries but they worked in different fields. Tagore was the first notable person who referred to Gandhi as ‘MAHATMA’ an appendage which struck to him throughout in later life.

Gandhi stayed in Shanti Niketan for a week. The reception arranged for him was a combination of art, love and simplicity. Gandhi did not like the use of hired servant for work and with Tagore permission he introduced the system of self-service to run the kitchen and for sweeping, cleaning and other jobs. But this system did not last long and was discontinued after Gandhi left.

Meeting Tagore

On his visit to Shanti Niketan, Gandhi went into the drawing room where Tagore was sitting on his sofa. The latter rose and offered Gandhi a seat beside him. But he decided to sit on the carpet on the floor. Tagore had a tall, stately figure well dressed with white hair and long beard while Gandhi was there, lean dressed in simple dhoti and shirt. This meeting therefore provided an amusing sight. However, the poet saw a great soul in the panny frame and the physical appearance was of little significance before inner greatness and grandeur.

Meeting Shradha Nanda

Gandhi Ji went to Haridwar to witness the Kumbha Festival where he was greatly disappointed to see the hypocrisy of the sadhus and the ignorance of the ordinary people who came to visit the festival. He took this opportunity to visit the Gurukul of Swami Shradhanand. In utter humility, he touched the feet of the Swami. An address of welcome was presented to Gandhiji who was addressed as ‘Mahatma’. This meeting led to close friendship between the two great holy person.

Sabarmati Ashram

After his return from South Africa in 1915, Gandhiji found an Ashram near Ahmedabad on the bank of the river Sabarmati. He called it Satyagraha Ashram which was latter known as Sabaramati Ashram. The inmates of this ashram took the vows of truth, celibacy, non-violence, non-stealing, non-possession control of the palate and total dedication to the service of the people. There were no servants in the Ashram. All were equal and all shared the same work. Sometime later than he opened this ashram, Gandhi admitted a family of untouchables. This was a revolutionary thing and there was opposition to it. The donation to the Ashram stopped. But Gandhiji kept his calm and then a miracle occurred. An unknown person gave him sufficient funds to run the ashram for an entire year. By then the storm subsided and even the orthodox people contributed in support of Gandhi's work.

In fighting untouchbility, Gandhiji faced considerable hardship and defied several taboos and hatred of rested interests. He called the untouchables 'Harijans' or children of God. This episode of entry of an untouchable family into the ashram gathered considerable support for Gandhi Ji from almost all Indian leaders.

Inter Caste Marriage Of His Son

Although Gandhi welcomed reforms in Hinduism, yet he proceeded with caution when it came to departing from age old customs. Gandhi's son Devdas fell in love with Lakshmi, the daughter of Rajagopalchari and wanted to marry her. But such inter caste marriages were not permitted those days. Rajagopalachari was a Brahmin while Gandhi a Vaisya. Again marriages were arranged by parents and young persons were not encouraged to choose their partners. But, in this case both parents had to agree on the conditions that they could marry after five years separation. So Devdas and Lakshmi waited for 5 years after which they got married in the presence of both happy fathers.

Gandhiji And Breakfast

Gandhi was in jail along with Vallabh Bhai Patel. He used to think about truth, non-violence, non-greed and so on. He would take ten dates immersed in water, as morning breakfast. Patel thought this was insufficient so one day he increased the number of dates to fifteen, thinking that Gandhi won't become aware of it. But Gandhi noted this and asked Patel to count dates. He did so and said what difference does make 10 or 15 dates make. Gandhi heard this, closed his eyes and began thinking. After a while he spoke Patel you have given me a new direction. You said there is hardly any difference between ten and fifteen. That makes me think that there should be hardly any difference between ten and five. From today, I will take only five dates.

One who thinks of non-greed and non-possession will think in terms of 'less and less'. A greedy man who has materialistic approach will think in terms of more and more and his desires will never be satisfied.

This is the difference between an ordinary person and a Mahatma.

Gandhi And Kasturba

Once Gandhi and Kasturba went some where. Their hosts had not seen Kasturba earlier. In the evening Gandhi was taken to address a gathering and Kasturba also accompanied him. Now Kasturba looked an old woman and organizers did not know that she was Gandhi's wife. So one man who rose to introduce Gandhi to the audience said, "We are glad that Gandhiji has come and are more fortunate that his mother has also come with him." Kasturba and Gandhi's secretary were greatly astonished. The secretary got panicky and thought that it was his mistake and he should have told the organizers about Kasturba. But Gandhiji remained calm and said, "My friend who introduced us just now has mistakenly spoken the truth. Kasturba my wedded wife has been to me like mother for the past few years." This was because Gandhi had taken the vow of brahmacharya and his relationship with Kasturba was no longer that of husband and wife.

Formation Of Natal Indian Congress

Gandhiji wanted to weld the hetrogenous Indian community into a disciplined organization. He therefore organized the Natal Indian Congress and himself framed the committe rules for its effective functioning. He made a rule that every member was to address another using the prefix of Mr. and smoking was not permitted. In the beginning, lots of enthusiasm was generated and members came forward with contributions and donations. Receipts were issued for every amount however small and proper accounts were maintained.

Committed Vegetarian

While in England, Vegetarianism became an article of faith for him so much so that he could risk his life for its sake. Once when he was laid up with an attack of bronchitis, the doctor advised him to take meat and beaf-tea and also warned that he would die if he did not do so.

Gandhi's reply was, "if it were God's will that I should die, I must die but I am sure it can't be God's will that I should break my oath." He did not break his oath, as he was under vow not to eat meat.

Such was the resolve of Gandhi Ji and his firm conviction for vegetarianism.

Travel By Third Class

On his return from South Africa to India towards the end of 1901, Gandhi came to Calcutta to attend the annual session of Indian National Congress. During his stay at Calcutta he took the decision to go round the country travelling by third class in order to feel the hardships faced by the III class passengers. During his train journey, Gandhi experienced the tremendous difficulties in third class. Thereafter, Gandhi Ji always travelled in third class while travelling in train.

Public Service

While in Natal, Gandhiji was deeply occupied in public service in the interests of his countrymen, he got a very sad news of death of his spiritual guide Raichandbhai. Gandhiji had no time to mourn his death. He wrote to a friend, 'I got the letter while I was at my desk. Reading it I felt grieved for a minute and then plunged immediately into work.' This showed how seriously Gandhiji took up public work as a moral duty and religions act. He had time for public service but not for himself. Service to the community was main engagement.

Gandhiji Cow's Milk

While in Calcutta Gandhiji came to know about the cruel treatment meted out to cows in extracting the last drop of milk from them. Gandhiji therefore decided to give up milk. He took this step for preventing cruelty to the cows.

Gandhiji And Gifts

Farewell meeting were arranged at several places when Gandhiji left Natal to come to India and costly presents were given to him and his wife. One of the gifts was a precious gold necklace worth fifty guineas meant for his wife. These costly gifts set Gandhiji thinking whether he had the right to keep them and this thought created a conflict in his mind and his family. It was difficult for him to return their gifts and more difficult to keep them. Since he was making efforts to shed worldly possessions how could he afford to keep their costly gifts. So he decided to create a trust of these gifts to be utilized by the Natal Indian Congress in their need.

Death Of Mother

Gandhi's mother Putlibai died when he was in England but the news of her death was not conveyed to him. When he returned to India from England his brother come to receive him at Bombay. Gandhi's first question was 'How is mother?' His brother somehow parried the question and diverted his attention towards another important matter. In the evening, Gandhi asked the same question 'How is mother?' His brother then could not hide the fact and he informed Gandhi about the death of mother in a very gentle manner. The news was a severe shock for Gandhi who loved his mother very much. But he kept his calm and mental composure and did not give into any wild expression of grief.

How Gandhi Treated A Leper

While in South Africa, Gandhi's house in Durban was an open house for all who came to get some help. He visited several of his law clerks to live with him as there were several rooms in the house. One day a leper came to the door begging. Gandhi brought him in, dressed his wounds. In consultation with Kasturba, he offered him shelter and care. Later he took him to the hospital as he lacked proper facilities for the care and treatment of the afflicted person for whom hospital was the proper place.

Meeting Students At Madras

This was a memorable occasion at madras railway station when a group of students came in search of Gandhi who was travelling by train with Kasturba. They searched all first and second class coaches but did not find him. At last, they found him in a third class coach at the end of the train. The students were greatly impressed by this moral example of renunciation by a great leader. They shouted with cries of appreciation 'Long live Mr. and Mrs. Gandhi'. They were both taken away to a waiting carriage driven by horses. The students out of admiration unyoked the horses and themselves pulled the cart in the streets on hero's march.

Encounter With A Cobra

While travelling through Harijan locations, one hot summer day, the meeting lasted from early morning to late evening. Gandhi was tired and Kasturba asked him to go inside a hut and relax. However, as it was hot inside she got a mat spread outside under a tree. A thin sheet was brought to cover his body. As darkness descended, Gandhi felt something soft at his side. He realized the situation and spoke in a soft voice, 'Do not panic and do not be afraid' and then he instructed the bystanders to lift the sheet carefully and take it away. When they did that they found a deadly long cobra. Kasturba uttered a silent prayer of thanks giving. Gandhi kept his composure and saved an impending tragedy.

Theft In Ashram

While in Sabarmati ashram, Kasturba small box of personal effects was stolen from the hut. Gandhi refused to call the police and expressed disappointment that there was something with Ba worth stealing. He was surprised to know that Ba had any such possessions. She explained that the box contained only clothing for the grand children. Gandhi remarked that grand children should take care of their own clothes. From then onwards Kasturba belongings were the smallest of anyone in the ashram. Gandhi believed in 'Aprigraha' which meant an attitude of non possession or minimum possession of things material.

Firm Resolve Of Gandhiji

Gandhi had read somewhere that in order to regain their health, frail people should avoid lentils and other legumes. When Kasturba fell seriously ill and become very weak, Gandhi advised her to do so. But she did not take his advice seriously and instead told him, "Why don't you give up lentils, before advising others?" Gandhi realized the weight of her argument even though she was only taunting him. He said, "Ok, I shall give up all this stuff for one year. Now what about you." Kasturba did not anticipate this and said, "oh, no no, you need not do this. I was only joking." But Gandhi was firm in his resolve and said, "You might be joking but you have taught me an important lesson. If I ask others to give up things I should first give up these things." Kasturba said, "I can't let you do this. You must take back your words." Gandhi replied, "How can I take back words which have left my lips." Thereafter, together they began their new diet plan and the condition of Kasturba improved considerably.

Guests Of Kasturba

While Gandhi was very strict about his rules and regulations for residents in the ashram, Kasturba was more lenient and loving.

Once a few young girls from a Mahila ashram came to visit Sevagram, where Gandhi and Kasturba lived along with other inmates. Earlier these girls had sought permission of Gandhi to visit the ashram. He had agreed and put the condition that they should bring own food.

When the girls come after finishing their work, they sat under a tree and began to eat their food. On seeing this, Kasturba enquired and was told about Gandhi's condition. She said, "you come along with me." She took them to the verandah of her hut and made them sit there and began distributing food to them.

Gandhi saw this and said, "what is going on here?" She said, "Don't tell me that our ashram is unable to feed a few guests!" He replied, "But there is no need for this, as I had already explained the conditions to them." Kasturba insisted, "You may explain whatever you like. But these young girls are my guests now and they can not go hungry."

Bapu simply smiled and went his way.

Gandhiji Without Rail Ticket

Once Gandhi was to travel by train, with his staff members. Before the train moved, he came to know that they were all without tickets. He called the station master and enquired. He said, "Sir, Mahapurush (great man) like you do not need ticket."

Gandhi said, "Is this how you allow so many 'Mahapurush' to travel without tickets." The tickets were then purchased for all.

Stickler For Time

Gandhi was a great stickler for time and was always punctual. Once a professor fixed and an appointment at 11:00 a.m. at his Wardha ashram. He reached the ashram much earlier and saw a man sweeping the courtyard. He told the man, "Go and tell Gandhiji that the professor has come to meet him." The man said, "Gandhi will meet you at 11:00 a.m." The professor said, "But you should go and tell him about my coming." The man did not go and said, "I have told you Gandhi will meet you at 11:00 a.m. After sometime, when it was 11.00 a.m., the same man stood before the professor and said, "I am Gandhi, I have come to meet you at 11.00 a.m."

The professor was greatly surprised to see that the great man was sweeping himself. This showed the sense of punctuality and the dignity of labour of Gandhi Ji.

Gandhi Ji And III Class

Gandhi used to travel in train by third class. Once someone asked, "Bapu why do you travel by third class?"

Gandhi promptly replied, "Because there is no IV class." This shows the ready wit and humility of Gandhi.

Humour Of Gandhi

Gandhiji used to gently slap a child whom he loved and this was noticed by Khan Abdul Gaffar Khan. He asked Gandhi, "Bapu you slap someone whom you love but you have never slapped me. This means you do not love me."

Gandhi looked at the huge physical frame of Gaffar Khan and remarked, "I do love you but I do not slap you because if you pay me back in the same coin, then I will be crushed."

All those present had a great laugh. Such was the humour of Gandhi.

Three Monkeys Of Gandhi Ji

Gandhi used to keep small statues of three monkeys in his room. The visitors found these monkeys a great source of surprise and amusement. These monkeys had different postures and Gandhi had kept them with a special purpose in mind. One monkey kept his eyes covered with both hands. The second monkey had his ears covered with both hands and the third monkey kept his mouth shut with his hands.

These monkeys conveyed the following messages:-

Do not see any evil.

Do not hear any evil.

Do not speak any evil.

Tact Of Gandhi Ji

Somebody asked Gandhi, “Is the Ramayana true or false?” It was a funny question. Gandhi thought for some time and then said, “I was not there, when the Ramayana was written!”

This shows Gandhi’s tact.

Ready Wit Of Gandhi

Gandhiji went to England to attend the round table conference. There he met King George V, at a reception. When he came out of the palace, a reporter asked him, “Mr. Gandhi, what did the king say about your dress?”

Gandhi was scantily dressed in a dhoti and a wrapper. He replied, “His majesty did not make any comment. After all he was wearing enough for the two of us!” Gandhi was a ready wit.

Tit For Tat

A critic of Gandhiji wrote a nasty poem on him and appended a note saying, “Mr. Gandhi you will find it useful.”

Gandhi read it removed the pin attached to it and returned the paper saying, “yes, I have kept the useful item.” This was a befitting reply to the critic.

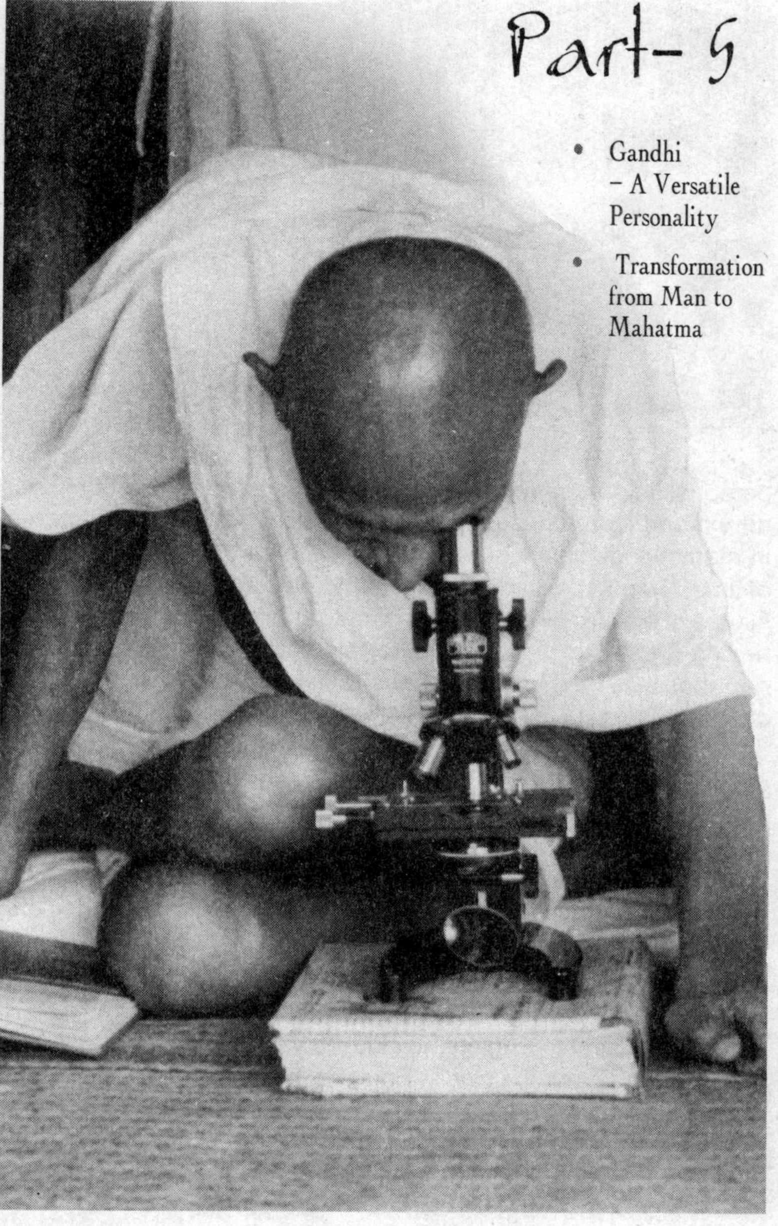

Part- 5

- Gandhi
  – A Versatile Personality
- Transformation from Man to Mahatma

Gandhi - A Versatile Personality

Gandhi has become a legend. He was a unique personality, a superman who performed great deeds, but he was an extraordinary unusual person as well, who took deep interest in many things considered small and ordinary. With the passage of time, Gandhi passed through many roles and guises at different stages of his life. First, he was a timid school boy, an obedient son having great love and respect for his parents then a passionate and possessive husband, an earnest but uninspired college student, an unsure young lawyer trying to earn some income for the family. After his return from South Africa, he became a self-assured lawyer who had earned the respect of the many. The experiences and experiments in South Africa made him more thoughtful, more mature, more wise, more forceful and more confident. The different roles which he played in his journey of life, depict various facets of his versatile personality, as mentioned in the following paragraphs:-

In The Role Of A Barrister

Gandhi was sent to England to study law, on the advice of a family friend. After 32 months stay in England, he became a barrister and returned to India. He started his legal practice in Bombay but was not successful. Gandhi, therefore, felt miserable. Luckily he got an offer to go to South Africa to work for an Indian company. This was literature assignment. After completing his assignment, Gandhi started practising in Durban Court. He noticed how the Indians were treated by the whites. He fought for the poor Indian labours and got them Justice. This made him popular among the Indian community and his legal practice flourished. His legal practice was based on truth and honesty. He never told untruth or tutored a witness for winning a case. He accepted the usual fee whether his client won or lost the case. Once while conducting a case, he came to know that his client was dishonest. He rebuked his client for the false case and asked the magistrate to dismiss the case. In the way, he built up a reputation for truth and honesty. Thus, the Judges as well as his colleagues respected him. In South Africa, his legal practice flourished for several years. At the beginning he set up an establishment in a lavish style but gradually he changed to simple life and identified himself with the poor Indian community. Thereafter, he gave up practice and dedicated himself to public service.

Gandhi condemned the high fees charged by lawyers in India. For the cases of the poor, he did not charge any fees. In other cases of public work he charged only the pocket expenses. He worked hard for each case, made a nominal charge, half of which he donated to build a charitable hospital. In South Africa, out of 70 cases, only one was lost. As a barrister, he was looked upon as the friend of this friendless.

His Own Barber

In South Africa, the white barber refused to cut Gandhi's hair due to colour hair. He bought a pair of clippers, went home and standing before the mirror, cut his own hair. In this act, he spoiled the front portion of his hair. When he went to the court, his clownish hair cut made his colleagues laugh. One asked in good humour, "What is wrong with your hair? Have rats nibbled at it last night?"

Afterwards, he used the scissors with the clippers. In his ashrams, the services of a barber were not utilized. The inmates cut the hair of one another, by turn. Gandhi used to cut the hair of ashram boys.

During his prison terms in South Africa, he would cut the hair of his co-prisoners with a pair of scissors and clippers. In India, when he travelled from village to village and could not find time to shave, then at times, he needed a barber's help, otherwise he acted his own barber.

The Great Scavenger

Gandhi learnt the art of scavenging in South Africa. His friends there would lovingly call him the great scavenger. While in England he admired sanitation and wanted to introduce that type of cleanliness in India.

In his house in Durban, commodes and chamber pots were used and Gandhi used to clear his own chamber pots. Sometimes, he would clear chamber posts of visitors also. He also taught his wife and young sons to do this work. In a South African jail, he would do a sweeper's work.

While touring some villages in India, he would personally supervise the scavenging work. He would also set an example by going to a village with bucket and broom. All scavenging work in his ashrams was done by the inmates and Gandhi guided them. His ashrams were kept clear and no dirt could be found there. He himself felt happy by doing cleaning work.

Instead of hating scavenging and to continue it as a forced cheap hired labour, he wanted to upgrade it as indispensable social work. He visited bhangi settlements and tell them that there was nothing bad or disgraceful in doing this work.

Gandhi described himself as a bhangi on several occasions. Sometime before his death, he stayed for some days in the sweeper's colony in Bombay and Delhi. He shared both lodging and food with them. He would advise them to avoid drinking and eating flesh. He would also tell, how scavenging could he done neatly, with the use of proper implements. He felt scavenging was a fine art and he did it without becoming dirty himself.

A Self-made Cook

While in England, Gandhi had difficulty in getting vegetarian food. He, therefore, hired a room and a stove and decided to cook himself. In this way, he saved on time and money.

In his ashrams in South Africa and India, he prescribed a simple menu for all without catering to the differing tastes and meals were cooked in a common kitchen. In his farm in Phoenix, he acted as the chief cook. He served as a cook for the marchers of satyagraha in South Africa. In a South African jail, he helped his co-prisoners in cooking.

As a cook, Gandhi could prepare rice, dal, vegetable soup, salads, bread, biscuits, chapattis, marmalade and cake etc. Gandhi considered cooking as an essential part of education.

Gandhi As A Doctor

Gandhi had a desire to qualify for the medical profession. Being a Vaishnara, the dissection of live animals stood in the way. Later, however, he did not like the allopathic system of medicine, he wanted new experimentation in the Ayurvedic system. Homeopathy did not attract him.

His great interest in healing process and his experiments in water and earth treatment, made him a naturopathy. He was influenced by the use of natural elements of water, earth, fresh air, sun's rays as aids in curing diseases. He also stressed the importance of fasting and proper diet. He made experiments in this natural farms of treatment on himself, wife and sons, and come out successful. In South Africa, he tried his methods on his friends and clients, to good results.

While his son suffered from typhoid in South Africa, he tried his nature cure treatment on him, even against medical advice and cured him by administering wet water packs and orange juice. On another occasion, he treated his wife also with nature cure methods.

Gandhi laid particular stress on keeping the bowl clean and for this he advised fasts, use of enema and regulation of diet. He found long walks useful for keeping fit. He also recommended breathing exercises. He was against pills and powder. He was interested for preventive measures than the curative ones. He also considered complete faith in God as a remedy for all troubles.

Gandhi knew that naturopathy had its limitations yet he advocated it especially for the poor masses of India. However allopathic drugs were not a taboo. During cholera outbreak in the ashram, he permitted vaccination. He himself was operated in jail for appendicitis on one occasion, he decided to devote one hour each day to sick patients in his ashrams as well as from the neighbouring area. In jail too he attended on his sick co-prisoners.

How He Worked As A Nurse

Gandhi had a desire for nursing from his childhood. After the school closed he would run home to nurse his ailing father. He gave him medicine, washed and dressed his wound and massaged his legs. In South Africa, he would devote sometime daily for nursing. When Gandhi's son got his arm fractured he dressed his wound for about a month. When his other son suffered from typhoid he nursed him for forty days. While nursing the sick he made the patient feel at ease and in peace.

Gandhi was more than a nurse to his patients whom he sponged, gave baths and enema and applied mud-poultice. He had no fear of getting infected. Once in South Africa, he gave shelter to a leper and dressed his ugly wounds and later took him to a hospital for proper treatment.

During Boer war and Zulu rebellion in South Africa, he raised an Indian ambulance corps and tended the sick and the wounded. Again during plague breakout, he helped the sick.

Gandhi nursed his wife and sons when they fell ill. Kasturba twice fell seriously ill in South Africa and doctors had no hope for her recovery. Gandhi nursed her with great patience and devotion. He acted as a mid-wife when Kasturba gave birth to her last son.

During Kasturba's last illness, when Gandhi was 75, he nursed her and provided much relief to her till end.

As A Shoe Maker

Gandhi learnt the craft of shoe making from his German friend in South Africa. He used to make sandals while in jail and would also teach shoe making to others in his ashram. He would use the hide of only those animals that died a natural death. He also learnt the art of tanning. He decried that tanners, sweepers and shoe-makers were despised and not given due regard in India and are also considered untouchables. In other counties, it is not so if a person chooses the profession of a tanner or a shoemaker. Gandhi tried to change there conditions.

Gandhi once presented a pair of hand-made sandals to General smarts in South Africa. The General had sent Gandhi in Jail. Several years later, the General having realized the greatness of Gandhi said, "I have worn them many a summer, though I feel that I am not worthy to stand in the shoes of so great a man."

As A Washer Man

In South Africa, Gandhi purchased a complete set of washing outfit along with a book on washing. He practiced the art of washing and also taught the same to Kasturba. He wanted to save the heavy washing bill of the washer man and also wanted to be self-reliant.

One day he washed a collar and ironed it and went to the court with the same collar which was over starched and badly ironed. Gandhi's colleagues made fun of him but Gandhi was least disturbed and said, "This is my first attempt on washing, but it does not matter. At least, it provided you with so much fun."

While Gandhi washed his own clothes he was not ashamed of washing others clothes. Once when he was the guest of a rich man he washed his dhoti along with the dhoti of his host also, as it was lying in the bath room. The host protested and said, "Bapuji what have you done?" Gandhi said, "Why? what is wrong in it? I am not ashamed of doing a bit for keeping things clean."

Gandhi cared much about cleanliness. He kept his dress clean all through life. He was a picture of cleanliness. He did not like shabby clothes. He kept his clothes spotlessly clean.

He Stitched Clothes

In jail Gandhi had to sew torn blankets and sew pieces of clothing given to him as part of hard labour.

He advised the use of small sewing machine to save much labour but he was not in favours of big machines displacing working hands. He did not want man to become slave of machine.

He could do needle work, sew his own kurta and his wife's blouses. While he was sewing he would also dictate letters to his secretary. After taking the vow of swadeshi he wore hand wowen clothes which were sewn by him or his co-workers.

Gandhi used to spin yarn on a charkha and then weave on a handloom. With the cloth this made, he would sew his own kurta. Later, he gave up the use of kurta and wore a loincloth and a wrap.

Spinner And Weaver

When Gandhi came to know about CHARKHA (the spinning wheel) he employed an expert spinner to teach its use to the inmates of his ashram. Soon he learnt to ply a charkha and would spin for sometime daily. He used to spin even while travelling in a train and also spin in public meetings, seated on a dais.

Gandhi advised the use of Khadi and wanted the poor to spin own yarn and become self-sufficient by using the cloth made by their own yarn. He wanted the villagers to ply charkha during their idle hours. He wanted the spinning mills and the spinning wheel to co-exist. During the freedom movement he inspired the whole country to wear khadi.

Once someone asked Gandhi his occupation and he replied, "I am a spinner, weaver and farmer". Due to the tyranny of the east India company, the wearing and cloth making industry of India was destroyed. India which used to export hand woven cloth, was compelled to import British made cloth. Our skilled craftsmen were reduced to poverty and made jobless. The weaving profession became disreputable. Indian became dependent on the import of foreign cloth.

Gandhi wanted to reverse this situation. He, therefore, wanted to revive hand-weaving. In order to popularize hand weaving he installed hand looms in his ashram at Sabarmati. All the inmates of the ashram wore clothes made on these handlooms. Gandhi himself worked on the looms for 4-5 hours daily. He was in favour of everybody learning spinning and weaving to stop the import of all foreign cloths and to make India self reliant. He also advised those engaged in this industry to bring about improvements in the process of spinning and weaving and in the quality of stuff so produced.

A Great Teacher

After his marriage at a young age. Gandhi tried to teach his wife who was illiterate but he failed as she lacked interest.

When he went to South Africa he found that most Indian there were not educated and did not know English. He advised them to learn English during their leisure time. Three young men, a barber, a clerk and a shopkeeper expressed readiness to learn and Gandhi went to their places to teach them. He taught them enough English to keep accounts and write their letters.

In South Africa, being very busy, Gandhi had no time to teach their sons. They used to walk with him to his office and he would teach them in Gujarati about some subjects. At Phoenix Settlement, he started a primary school for the children of the inmates. He acted as the head teacher while his co-workers assisted him. Gandhi did not teach with books and laid stress on building of character. The students were trained to do some manual work and appreciate music.

In Sabarmati ashram, arts subjects were taught through the vernacular. English was a secondary language. Gandhi advocated co-education, as he wanted students to rid of sex mentality. The youngsters were taught to learn some occupational work, so spinning and weaving etc. was also taught. Gandhi taught orally through stories and choice selections of English literature.

Gandhi thought that students should be developed into healthy, honest, intelligent and upright young men able to earn their livelihood instead of mere literates. He was against the use of any corporal punishment. He urged them to compete in games. He emphasised that students must learn some handicraft so that they are not ashamed of manual labour. Gandhi was also in favour of adult man education in order to remove their helplessness and general ignorance.

An Excellent Writer

Gandhi wrote numerous articles and speeches on various subject most of them were later converted into books. His style of writing was forceful but simple, precise and clean. He did not use flowery language. He wrote in Gujarati but also expressed himself in excellent English.

His first attempt in writing was a small booklet *'London Guide'* written for Indian students studying in UK. Then he wrote two pamphlets about the general conditions of Indians in Natal. These were *'An appeal to every Briton'* and *'The Indian Franchise'*. Another pamphlet about Indians in South Africa, entitled *'Green Pamphlet'* angered the Europeans there and he was maltreated on account of that.

Gandhi described his experiments in diet and nature cure in a small booklet *'Key to health'*. This was based on his articles written in the 'Indian opinion' under the heading *'Guide to Health'*. This book become very popular and was translated into several Indian and European languages. His other small booklets include *'Hind Swaraj'* which is a severe criticism of modern civilization.

'Constructive program' a booklet on nation building, *'Sarvodaya'* which was adapted into Gujarati from Ruskins *'Until this last'*. He

also wrote *'Songs from the prison'* which contained poems of some saint poets of India, translated into English, when he was in jail.

Gandhi wrote his autobiography in Guajarati in a simple but forceful style. In English translation *'The story of my Experiments with truth'* has been adjudged a good piece of literature. It has been translated into all main Indian languages and several European languages. He also wrote books for children.

A vital part of his writings consists of thousands of letters, which are informative and instructive. He also wrote short sketches of prominent people in the Guajarati Journal Indian opinion and also mentioned about incidents, examples from the Indian epics and the lines of great man.

His writings laid emphasis on truth, non-violence and other moral values and he made his ideas simple and easily understandable. That is why his writings touched readers hearts. His manuscripts seldom needed any modifications. He attributed this to the spiritual discipline. He believed that literature had value only if it helped people to rise upwards. As a writer truth was his guiding star.

Role Of A Farmer

Gandhi was born in a bania family but as he grew he took great interest in farming. He loved to grow and water the plants at home. But his farming skill really blossomed when he went to South Africa and set up a big farm. Gandhi tilled the land, grew vegetables and fruits and built up cottages where he lived with his family and co-workers.

As a result of about ten years of farm life in South Africa, Gandhi gained good knowledge and experience of farming process. He believed that a farmer should be energetic, self-reliant and resourceful. To begin with, he did not use the plough, used hoe, and taught other to use it.

Gandhi believed in self-help, self-reliance and proper use of labour force. He favoured organic manure which can be prepared with cow dung, night soil, peelings of vegetables etc. Such a manure could be produced without any capital. He was also more in favour of cattle plough and hand work.

He also advocated copulative farming which included collective cattle farming also. He advised good proper care of the animals and a common proper greasing ground. He considered cow as the most valuable animal and laid great stress on its protection. In his ashram he maintained model cow-shed where animals were given good care and treatment.

Gandhi wanted to raise the income of poor peasants who remained without work for a long period during which he accommended spinning for women and wearing for men to increase their earnings. He wanted good dwellings, proper clothing, proper education and health requirements for the poor peasants. He also wanted that land should belong to the tilling farmer and not to the absent land lord. He believed that Indians salvations lay through the farmer as our 75 per cent of the population consisted of agriculturist.

A Fearless Jail Bird

Gandhi fought against injustice and tyranny throughout his life, without any fear. He launched satyagraha and mass civil disobedience movement and was jailed several times. He spent 6 years and 10 months in prison and was arrested eleven times. In some cases, his punishment was reduced.

It was in South Africa that Gandhi was sent to prison for the first time for a period of two months, where he was lodged with other prisoners. In jail he noticed that European prisoners were served better food than Indians. He protested, made a complaint and succeeded in getting a better deal. In jail he helped in cooking food and also volunteered to do manual labour. He also stopped taking tea and started taking dinner before sunset.

On several times in South Africa, he was awarded hard labour and taken to prison in handcuffs. He was kept under bad insanitary conditions along with the worst type of confirm convicts. Jail life was full of hardships and without even basic luring facilities. He had to sew torn clothes, clean lavatories, polish iron doors and rule floors etc. He suffered all these hardships bravely and with peace of mind.

When confined in a solitary call, he had nothing but a loin cloth on. While detamed in a palatial building he asked the jail superintendent to remove all furniture and extra pots and pans. He used one iron cot and a few utensils.

Gandhi did not feel bitter in jail he felt as happy as a bird. He read lot of books in jail, which he was unable to do when outside because of his numerous activities. He also spun for a few hours every day and also took brisk walks. He also wrote books while in jail. He observed the jail discipline did whatever work was given to him and observed all good jail regulations. Gandhi maintained his self-respect while imprisoned. He also cared and helped his colleagues in jail. He also regularly prayed in jail.

A Leader Of The Masses

A shy timid young had involved in public service during his stay in South Africa. When he returned to India and plunged in the Indian freedom struggle, he become a leader of the masses.

South Africa served as the training ground in his ascent to leadership. In South Africa, he fought for the human rights of Indians, besides for his own self-respect and dignity. He called a public meeting of the Indians and made his first public speech in which he exhorted them to forget their differences, be honest and inculcate clean habits and proper behaviour. He listened to their grievances fought for them and suffered handships for doing public service. Inturn, they admired and respected him, followed his advice and worked under his guidance and accepted him as the leader of the Indian community in South Africa. During his twenty years stay there he guided and helped the Indian settlers in spite of personal misery and hardships suffered in the process.

On his final return to Indian from South Africa, he toured all over India, established close contact with the masses and studied thin problems. He met and interviewed thousands of persons and worked tirelessly for 18 to 20 hours a day, talking to people and collecting information from them. He addressed thousands of public meetings and laid emphasis on discipline, non-violence and moral values in order to prepare them for the fight for India's freedom. People listened to Gandhi revered him and took part whole-heartedly in his movements, on a mass scale. His historic DANDI MARCH for salt making was an act of bravery which caught the imagination of the people who flocked to the roadside to pay respect and lend their support to the unarmed great man who had the courage to break the unjust law made by the British rules. The success of his symbolic act made a dramatic impact which resulted in a nationwide challenge to the low. The whole country burst into a fire of protest and mass meetings took place in all the cities.

The civil disobedience movement thus generated raised Gandhi to the apex of his political career and he become the topmost leader of the Indian nation.

Gandhi was a practical leader. He first practiced himself what he preached to others. He was a fearless leader, prepared to sacrifice himself before he asked others 'Do or Die'. He justified his choice of non-violence but preferred violence to cowardice. He attached greater importance to soul force than brute force. He admired virtues of bravery, patriotism, endurance and self-sacrifice in his non-violent fights.

As the tallest leader of the Indian freedom movement, his mantra was 'Do or Die'. He was a practical hard task master and never raised false hopes in his followers, as they would have to face hardships and make lot of sacrifices. By self-sacrifice and suffering, he appealed to the heart of his opponents.

Truly he was a leader with mass appeal and an uncrowned king of India.

A Man Of True Religion

Gandhi had firm faith in God and believed in true religion, broad based and universal. His concept of religion was neither narrow nor sectarian. He believed that true religion should pervade all our actions and it means a universal belief in an orderly moral governance of the universe and human nature.

Gandhi believed that it was foolish for the followers of one religion to say, “Ours is the only true religion and all other are false”. He had studied several religions and could explain the basic tenets of Hinduism, Islam, Christianity, Sikhism and Buddhism etc. He could easily quote from the sayings of other religions. He often attended services at churches.

Born in a Hindu family, he believed in the philosophy of Hinduism. However, it was his conviction that all great faiths of the world are true and God-ordained. Thus he had respect for all religions. He believed that religions is one tree with many branches.

Gandhi believed that there is no religion higher then truth and righteousness and without moral basis, one ceases to be religious. He condemned social evils like untouchability, child marriage and other meaningless rituals etc. He preferred the worship of the formless but did not denounce idol worship become he thought that those who worship idols, worship not the stone but the God who resides in it.

Besides scriptures of Hinduism he also read scriptures of other religions as well. He did not make distinction between places of worship of various religions. He loved to pray and made it a part of his life. Without prayer he found his life dull and vacant. He believed that prayer is necessary for the soul and found his peace through prayer. Gandhi claimed to be a man of prayer and whenever he had some temporary despair, he got rid of it through prayer. He woke up early before sunrise and offered his prayer every morning and evening.

Prayer was a daily exercise for him and he stick to it, whether on land or sea or moving in a train or ship. He could deny himself food but could not pass a day without saying his prayer. For him, prayer was not a mere lip service but a living faith in the Almighty. It was not to please God, but to purify ones own self.

In his own words Gandhi says, “I could not live for a single second without religion.” His spirit of public service, polities and other activities were derived from his religious conviction. To him, religion meant being bound to God who rules your every breath.

Gandhi truly had a life based on religion. His faith in God was unshakable and he died with Gods name on his lips.

In view of the observation made in the preceding paras, it may well be concluded that Gandhi was the rarest of the rare human being who had the privilege and an extraordinary capacity to play various roles appropriately in different circumstances and stages of his life span.

It appears incredible how in so many things he took interest and he did so thoroughly and with ease. In the history of mankind it may be extremely difficult to find any other human who could match his performance. While he performed great deeds he was equally adept in dealing with what may be considered as small things of life. It is astounding and admirable to know how Gandhi functioned in a variety of roles, apart from public service and politics.

He was indeed a superman.

A Thought

“The highest honour that my friends can do me is to enforce in their own lives the programmer that I stand for or to resist me to their utmost if they do not believe in it.”

M.K. Gandhi

Transformation from Man to Mahatma

Gandhi was born as an ordinary child, without any silver or golden spoon in his mouth, without a spiritual halo around his head. As a child, he did not exhibit exceptional intellectual ability or any unusual trait of miraculous nature. Physically, not very strong, he was shy by nature and afraid of thieves and ghosts. He did not excel in studies either at school or college.

Married at a preposterously early age of thirteen, he pitied himself later, as marriage meant nothing to him, at that stage. But he was passionately fond of his wife and used to think of her even at school. Sometime later, after marriage, he became slave of carnal desire and the thought of meeting her wife, during the early period, was unbearable to him. Under the influence of a friend, he started meat eating and smoking and also visited a brothel although he did not commit any sin there. He also lied to hide the fact of meat eating.

As a student, he was mediocre, used to be very shy and avoided all company. He literally ran back home as soon as the school was closed. He was even afraid, lest anyone should poke fun at him. At high school, he was not regarded as dunce and even won prizes, but he himself did not have any high regard of his ability. His stay in England where he went to study law, was not marked by any distinction. He retained his shyness throughout his stay in

England. His last effort to make a public speech in England, on the eve of his departure for home, failed miserably.

The above picture of Gandhi depicts him as an ordinary mortal, to start with. However, the same ordinary man, in his later life, roar to become a colossus of Indian social and political scenario. He fought against the mighty British empire, where sun never set and became the tallest personality of the Indian freedom movement. The same ordinary person, by virtue of his gradual but determined progress, in the purity of thought, in the strength of his character and by fractions love, truth, non-violence and self restraint, rore to the moral heights of a MAHATMA (GREAT SOUL).

When he indulged in childish pranks of stealing, lying, smoking casually, meat eating etc., he acted as an ordinary man. Like a large majority of human beings, he was also greatly affected by carnal desire. But when he thought over his weaknesses, he not only released their evil consequences, but also conquered these passions and fully discarded them. While leaving bad habits, like smoking and stealing etc. may not be considered great achievements, controlling the carnal desire in thought, speech and action was indeed an indomitable task and the greatest victory. This was such a great feat, which even several holy men, even some rishi's of ancient time, could not accomplish. Victory over the most powerful sexual instinct has been described as the greatest of all victories. It was then that he truly acquired and deserved the title of MAHATMA.

Gandhi's life was rooted in ancient ethical traditions. Love for truth, service and non-violence got imprinted on his mind from a very young age. His life indeed was a perpetual pursuit for truth and non-violence. His life in South Africa became a practicing field for the implementation, upgradation and perfection of his ideals of service, love, truth, non-violence, tolerance, absence of hatred, fight against injustice, human rights, dignity and self-respect and many more moral and social values. His life and work in the difficult and hostile terrains of South Africa, paved the way for him to transform himself from Man to Mahatma. The racial turning point in his life came, when while travelling in a train in South Africa, he was forcibly thrown out of a first class compartment due to racial discrimination. It was then that he made a difficult resolve to stay back and fight against injustice, hatred and racial discrimination. He waged a relentless war against there evils prevailing in South Africa and came out successful. When Gandhi left South Africa at the age of 45, he had already grown into a full-fledged, self confident and widely respected personality. He had, by then, experimented with and practically adopted in his life, various street disciplines with regard to truth, non-violence, good conduct, love for mankind, public service, food, ethics and morality and many more alike. He preached and practiced all these in later life. By then, the real achievements of truth, non-violence and celibacy had been made. He had given up the pleasures of sex and the palate, he was without lust and greed, he had discarded unnecessary wealth and material possessions and had no desire for any gain not necessary for living.

By love, non-violence, service and renunciation he became a saint as great as Budha. He was a true servant, as well as the uncrowned king of India. He became a BAPU (Father) for the teeming millions and the *'Father of the Nation'*. None else in the Indian history could achieve there lofty distinctions.

The year 1906, may be rightly designated as a milestone in the life of Gandhi Ji. It was then that he experienced a deep inner spiritual awakening, to dedicate his whole life to the service of the community. He took the vow of 'BRAHMACHARYA' at that time his freedom began with it. He kept his vow untill death. It was a very daunting task but it came to him spontaneously and became a matter of ever-increasing joy. The irresistible attraction for brahmacharya drew him to view woman as the MOTHER OF MAN. And also impelled him towards the service of the country and the mankind. For him, brahmacharya was the highest goal which he could achieve because of his firm faith in God. This achievement alone brought a great change in him. This was the cause of the greatest transformation which paved the way for him from man to MAHATMA.

With his vow of brahmacharya, Gandhi stepped out of the narrow confines and attachments of the biological family and to embrace the vastness of entire human kind as his own. It was also in the same year, Gandhi opened the path of emancipation for the suffering humanity with his firm adherence to truth and non-violence. A new concept was born, as a result of his vow of brahmacharya. He named it as 'SATYAGRAHA'.

A shy, timid, who as a child did not exhibit an exceptional ability, grew into a young man of strong will and determination. As he marched forward on the moral path of truth, non-violence, love and service, he fought against injustice and racial discrimination in South Africa. In his home country, he fought the mightiest British Empire, with the non-violent means of 'SATYAGRAHA' and got independence for his countrymen. From the ordinary, he became exceptional, exemplary and extra-ordinary; from a physical weakling, he rose to become a spiritual force and from man to MAHATMA. His life was a journey from imperfection to perfection - which only a human being of rare acumen could attain.

Gandhi was not born great, neither was greatness thrust upon him, but, undoubtedly, he toiled and triumphed to achieve greatness of a rare kind. As rightly said by Dr. S. Radhakrishanan the first President of the Indian Republic, "A great teacher appears once a while. Several centuries may pass by without the advent of such a one."

Such a teacher and great man was Gandhi. He was BAPU for the teeming millions of India.

He was 'Father of the Nation'.

He was the uncrowned king of our country.

He was the greatest man of the twentieth century.

He was really a MAHATMA (Great Soul). Who stands out in the history of human civilization as a great prophet of love, truth and non-violence. He was the shining example of how one man could change the course of history.

It is most unfortunate that while his figure remains in lifeless photographs and portraits, dumb statues and dim memories, his principles, percepts and practices have been mostly forgotten.

A Thought

"I am but a seeker after TRUTH.

I am a humble but very earnest seeker of TRUTH"

M.K. Gandhi

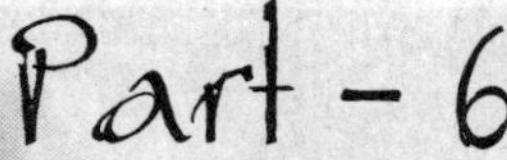

Part - 6

- Martyrdom of Gandhi Ji
- Tributes to Gandhi Ji

Rajghat

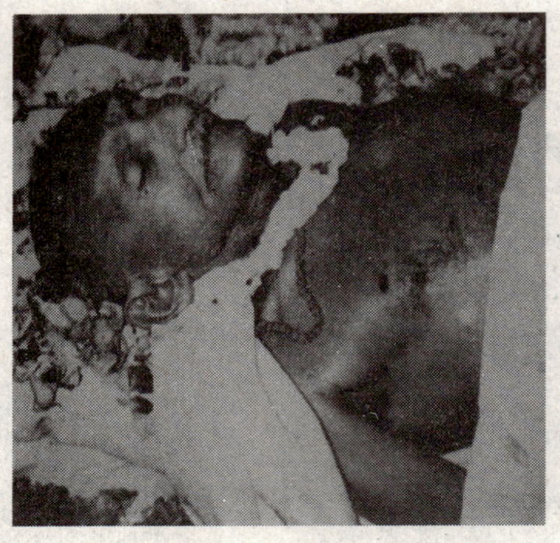

Martyrdom of Gandhi Ji

"The noblest figure of modern history."

An atribute to Gandhi Ji

Gandhi Ji's death on Janurary 30, 1948 was a great paradox. An apostle of peace, the greatest rotary of Ahimsa after Lord Budha and Mahavira, who had love for all and hatred towards none, fell a victim to an assassin's bullet and attained martyrdom of the rarest kind.

It seems that Gandhi had made a prophet about the manner of his death. When his assassin pumped buttets in Gandhi's chest, the latter fell down with God's name on his lips and breathed last. On the night of January 29, 1948, less than twenty hours before he was shot dead, he had uttered the following words:-

"If someone were to end my life by putting a bullet through me, and I breathed my last taking God's name, then alone would I have made good my claim."

Some of the words said earlier by Gandhi Ji, about his death, are as follows:-

"I do not want to die of a creeping paralysis of my faculties, a defeated man. An assassin's bullet may put an end to my life."

In this context, some more words are quoted below:-

"I am not achieving for martyrdom, but if it comes in my way in the prosecution of what I consider to be the supreme duty in defence of the faith I hold....I shall have earned it."

There is no doubt that Gandhi Ji had really earned his martyrdom which also came in his way in the performance of his duty. After his death, Gandhi Ji did not want his body to be taken out in a procession. He wanted to be cremated where he had died. He did not want to be reborn. But in case of rebirth, he wanted to be born as an untouchable, so that he would share their sorrows, sufferings and affronts inflected on them.

Tributes to Gandhi Ji

In the decades of history of Indian freedom movement, Gandhi had emerged as an icon, the tallest Indian idol who was honoured with the title of 'MAHATMA' and the 'Father of our Nation'. It is difficult to define of our Nation. It is difficult to define the greatness of such a personage whose name captured the spirit of India. He epitomizes the values which are difficult to come by in the present times.

Naturally, therefore, their was an upsurge of tridents not only from India but also from across the seas when Gandhi was assassinated. In order to acquaint the readers with the great regard, respect and admiration evoked from all corners of the world, we have summarised below some of the prominent tributes to the Mahatma.

Pt. Jawaharlal Nehru, the then Prime Minister of India described Gandhi Ji as the light that illumined India for many years and would illumine this country for a thousand years later. That light represented the eternal truths, reminding us of the right path away from error and took this country to freedom. He described Gandhi's death as a terrible blow to millions and millions in India.

Sri Rajagopalachari, the then Governor Ceramal of India said, *"No one could die a more glorious death than Mahatma Gandhi."*

A summary of some other prominent tributes is as follows:-

His death was described as supreme scarifies.

He was hailed as teacher, prophet, apostle of truth, love and peace, spiritual inspirer, undying influences, the purest spiritual flame, the liberator of community.

He was described as the greatest man of our times, but simple as a child.

He instilled dignity and self-respect in Indian politics.

He left a permanent impress on the minds and loves of humanity.

He sacrificed his life for Indian unity.

The greatest man of India where actions were based on bed-rock of moral values.

A zealous champion of women's cause.

He was such a great man who is born only once in many centuries.

He personified the essence of true religion. His achievements were greater than those of kings and saints.

A man of destiny, warrior, prophet and saint and unique in world history.

An outstanding son of mankind and architect of Indian freedom.

A great light and the greatest man of his time.

One of the greatest reformers and nation-builders of the world.

The Messiah of this age with inspiring teachings.

Full of love and gentleness, he completely eschewed hatred.

A solitary and yet shining beacon.

He was declared as the greatest Christian saint at a Christian conference.

His was a life of service to all.

He died a noble and memorable death which stunned all lovers of peace.

Champion of the weak, who changed the course of modern history.

Harbinger of peace who gave his life for humanity.

Noblest teacher and martyr to a great cause.

One of the greatest men in history.

His death was the greatest tragedy.

He lived and died for peace.

The greatest servant of humanity who gave his life for human service.

Timeless symbol of love and rectitude, the bulwark of world peace and liberty.

Universal brother, lover and friend who stood out head and shoulders above contemporaries.

A divined inspired saint, who left an indelible impression of goodness.

His death was an international tragedy.

He was a light to the whole world.

His noble life was inspiration to all.

The prince of peace whose loss affects all humanity.

A leader of international stature-and spokesman for the conscience of all mankind.

A prophet ahead of the times whose spirit reached for the stars.

He truly walked with God and his goodness made him great.

Not simply great but good. He belongs to the ages.

One of the saviours of the mankind.

A kind leader of the masses who died a martyr to liberty.

A moral leader of all humanity and a symbol of oppressed peoples' liberty.

Sublime example of sacrifice.

A leader of all peace lovers.

The greatest history builder of India.

The noblest figure of modern history.

A great patriot, who did not die.

Saintly crusader of peace and a leader of humanity.

He symbolized highest ideals of his people.

The only modern saint and prophet and the spirit to enlighten mankind.

Irreparable loss to mankind.

Messenger of peace and freedom.

Prophet of peace and great pacifist.

India's immortal son.

The great apostle of peace.

The most remarkable man.

Friend of the poorest, lowliest and the lost whose greatness belonged to the history.

Keystone of the arch of peace and martyr in the cause of Justice.

Example of unselfish devotion to the cause of humanity.

General SMUTS, the President of South Africa in 1914, who was the toughest opponent of Gandhi, who later became his admirer and wanted to salute him, described him as follows:-

'....a greatness in whose shoes I am not worthy to stand.'

Shri G.K. Gokhale, the great Indian leader had very high estimation and admiration for Gandhi Ji. At the Lahore session of Indian National Congress, he said as follows:-

"Gentlemen, it is one of the privileges of my life that I know Mr. Gandhi intimately and I can tell you that a purer, a nobler and a braver and a more exalted spirit has never moved on this earth."

This he said when Gandhi was young and alive. Gokhale was not alive when Gandhi died and his personality had reached the peak of perfection. Had he been alive their, one can imagine, he would have paid the highest tribute to the MAHATMA.

The martyrdoms of Gandhi Ji was mourned not only by millions and millions in India but also by millions across the world. The homage paid to the Mahatma was unique and the rarest in the annals of world history.

"The future generations will wonder if the kind of him ever lived in flesh and blood."

– Albert Einstein